THE ECONOMY OF AFRICA

By the same author on the African economy:

Analyse du sous-développement en Afrique noire. PUF, Paris, 1968.

Économie et enseignement à Madagascar. IIEP, Paris, 1976.

Vivre et survivre dans les villes africaines (co-editor with I. Deblé). PIF, Paris, 1981.

Nourrir les villes africaines (co-editor). L'Harmattan, Paris, 1985.

Les Afriques de l'an 2000 (editor). Special edition of *Afrique contemporaine*, 1988.

Les Tiers Nations en mal d'industrie (co-editor with J. de Bandt). Economica, Paris, 1988.

Économie du développement. Dalloz, Paris, 1989.

Urbanisation et dépendance alimentaire en Afrique subsaharienne (in collaboration with J. Coussy and O. Sudrie). SEDES, Paris, 1990.

Intégration régionale et ajustement structurel en Afrique (co-editor with J. Coussy). Ministry of Development and Co-operation, Paris, 1992.

Économie de l'Afrique. Éditions la Decouverte, Paris, 1993.

L'Afrique des incertitudes (co-editor with G. Pourcet and S. Quiers-Valette). PUF, Paris, 1994.

Économie politique internationale et mondialisation. Economica Poche, Paris, 1997.

La zone franc à l'heure de l'euro. Karthala, Paris, 1999.

Un bilan de la prospective africaine (co-editor with O. Sudrie). MAE, Paris, 2001.

La Côte-d'Ivoire à l'aube du XXI siècle (co-editor with G. Tapinos and P. Vimard). Karthala, Paris, 2001.

Les Économies en développement à l'heure de la régionalisation (editor). Karthala, Paris, 2003.

THE ECONOMY OF AFRICA

PHILIPPE HUGON

PROTEA BOOK HOUSE
PRETORIA
2004

The Economy of Africa
Philippe Hugon

First English edition, first impression 2004

Protea Book House
PO Box 35110, Menlo Park, 0102
protea@intekom.co.za

Typography and design by HOND BK
Reproduction by PrePress Images, Pretoria
Printed and bound by Paarl Print, Cape Town
Cover photograph © Horst Klemm, courtesy of
Mapungubwe Museum, University of Pretoria

ISBN 1-86919-027-0

Acknowledgements

The publisher would like to thank Dr Evert van Dijk for his invaluable participation in the editing of the English translation.

We are grateful to the French Institute of South Africa (IFAS) and the French Embassy, without whose support this publication would not have been possible.

Contents

List of abbreviations

ACP	African, Caribbean, Pacific
ANC	African National Congress
AU	African Union
AZT	Azidothymidine
BAD	(*Banque Africaine de Développement*) African Development Bank
BECP-level	(*Brevet Élémentaire du Premier Cycle*) In the French school system, a certificate obtained for the first four years of secondary education.
CEMAC	Central African Economic and Monetary Committee
CEPII	(*Centre d'Études Prospectives et d'Informations Internationales*) Institute for Research on the International Economy
CERED	(*Centre d'Études et de Recherche Démographique*) Centre for Demographic Research and Study
CFA	African Financial Community
CGEM	Calculated General Equilibrium Models
CIF	Cost, Insurance, Freight
CILSS	International Committee Fighting Against Drought in the Sahel
COMESA	Common Market for Eastern and Southern Africa
DFS	Decentralised Financing Systems
DRC	Democratic Republic of Congo
EAC	East African Community
ECA	Economic Commission for Africa
ECOWAS	Economic Community of West-African States
EDI	Economic Development Indicator
EEC	European Economic Community
EPA	Economic Partnership Agreement
EU	European Union
FIDES	(*Fonds d'investissement de développement économique et social*) Investment Fund for Social and Economical Development
FNUAP	(*Fonds des Nations Unies pour la Population*) United Nations Population Fund
FOB	Free on Board
GDP	Gross Domestic Product
GNP	Gross National Product
HDI	Human Development Indicator

HIPC	Highly-Indebted Poor Countries
HPI	Human Poverty Indicator
IMF	International Monetary Fund
LDC	Least-Developed countries
MAF	Multi-Fibre Arrangement
MNC	Multinational Corporation
NEPAD	New Partnership for Africa's Development
NGO	Non-governmental Organization
OAU	Organisation for African Union (now the African Union)
ODA	Overseas Development Assistance
OIC	Indian Ocean Commission
ONCAD	(*Office National de Coopération et d'Assistance pour le Développement*) National Office for Co-operation and Assistance for Development
OPEC	Organisation of Petroleum Exporting Countries
PDCI	(*Parti Democratique de Côte d'Ivoire*)Democratic Party of Ivory Coast
PPP	Purchasing-Power Parity
PRGF	Poverty Reduction and Growth Facility
PRI	(*Pays à revenu intermédiaire*) Countries with intermediary income
PZS	Priority Zone of Solidarity
RDA	(*Rassemblement Démocratique Africain*) African Democratic Rally
SADC	Southern African Development Community
SAP	Structural Adjustment Policy
SARF	Structural Adjustment Reform Facilities
SMEs	Small and Medium Enterprises
SMME	Small, Micro and Medium Enterpises
SSA	Sub-Saharan Africa
UNCTAD	United Nations Conference on Trade and Development
UNDP	Untited Nations Development Programme
UNESCO	United Nations Educational, Scientific and Cultural Organisation
UNHCR	United Nations High Commission for Refugees
VAT	Value-Added Tax
WAEMU	West African Economic and Monetary Union
WTO	World Trade Organisation

MAP 1: THE NINE MAJOR ECONOMIC REGIONS IN SUB-SAHARAN AFRICA

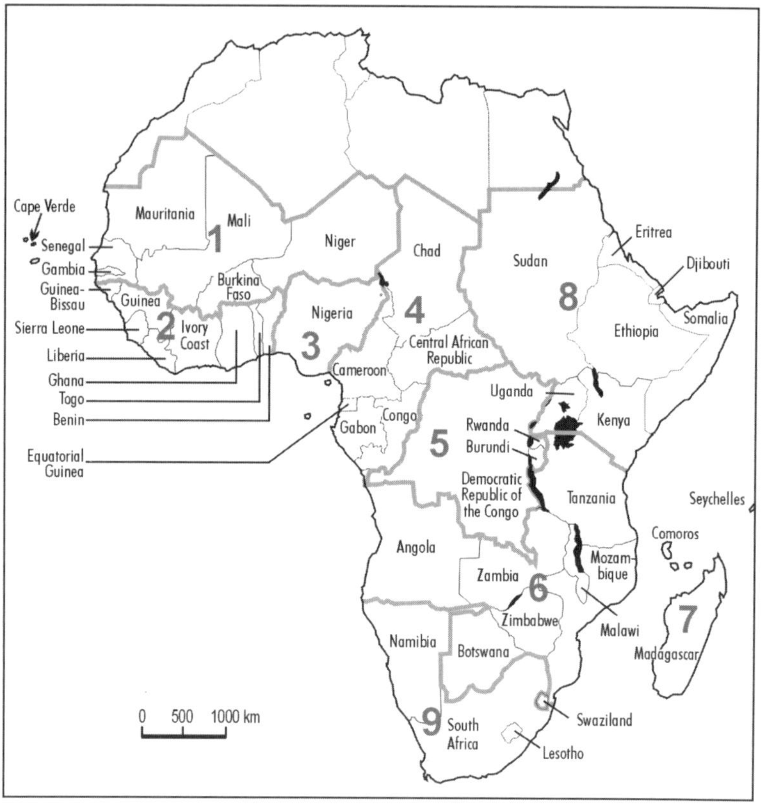

1. Sudan-Sahelian Africa; International Committee Fighting Against Drought in the Sahel (CILSS)
2. Humid and sub-humid western Africa
3. Nigeria
4. Central Africa; Central African Economic and Monetary Committee (CEMAC)
5. Economic Community of the Great Lakes countries
6. Sub-humid and semi-arid southern Africa; Southern African Development Community (SADC)
7. Indian Ocean; Indian Ocean Commission (OIC)
8. Eastern Africa; East Sahel
9. South Africa

INTRODUCTION

It is difficult to write a book about African economies for two main reasons.

Firstly, how does one explain the main issues when, even if one is limited to sub-Saharan Africa (SSA), the subcontinent is a territory of contrasts? In this book, the term "Africa" refers to sub-Saharan Africa, including South Africa. There are nine main regions (see Map 1 and Table 1, pages 8 and 10). Thirty-five of the 48 countries each have fewer than 10 million inhabitants and 15 are landlocked. The GDP of sub-Saharan Africa is almost the same as that of the Netherlands or of Mexico (US$370bn in 2003). All together, sub-Saharan Africa had close to 700 million inhabitants in 2003, representing 10 per cent of the global population, one per cent of global GDP, 1.3 per cent of global exports and less than one per cent of global industrial added value. Continental Africa's share in the global GDP, expressed in parity with its purchasing power, has decreased with a third between 1950 and 2000. Its share in global exports has been divided by three (BAD, OCDE, 2002). Sub-Saharan Africa represents 58 per cent of the African GDP (38 per cent when excluding South Africa). The second reason is more fundamental. One has to consider whether it is a matter of applying the instruments of economic analysis to this continent; or rather of questioning economic categories based on African particularities. Is there, for an economist, an *Africanist specificity*; or is there, for an Africanist, an *economic legitimacy*? Should an economist give greater importance to long-term accumulation systems and crises, or rather to the coherent frameworks of market balances (or imbalances) through the functioning of prices (or quantities)?

The subject of development economics does not only involve the application of universal tools of economic analysis (management of scarcity, allocation of resources under constraint) to a particular field; it also questions those tools required to open up the "black box" of social structures; and presents a long-term perspective. In this publication, the centrality of macroeconomics, albeit necessary for coherence sake, will be set against a historic perspective (part one); *macroeconomic analysis*, allowing an understanding of the behaviour of agents, is linked to *organisations* and *institutions* in a socio-political context (part two); and *political economy* debates will take into account the multiplicity of current tendencies and stakes, allowing for the definition of several *perspectives* (part three).

TABLE 1: MAIN INDICATORS OF AFRICA'S NINE MAJOR REGIONS (2000)

		2002 GDP (billion US $)	Per capita GDP (US $)		Current balance of payments (billion US $) Exports		Imports		External debt (billion US $)		GDP annual growth rate (%)		Total population (m)	Annual population growth rate	Artificial fertility index
			1989	1998	1990	1998	1990	1998	1990	2002	1965–1980	1990–1998	2000	1960–1990	1990
CEDEAO	*1. Sahel*	11.5	758	300	2.2	1.8	3.2	5.0	11.1	21	–	3.0	46.0	2.5	6.5
CEDEAO	*2. West Africa*	21.5	946	380	4.4	8.3	5.1	9.3	29.7	41.8	6.3	3.0	63.5	3.1	6.8
CEDEAO	*3. Nigeria*	41.0	1160	370	13.7	15.6	5.7	6.4	36.1	38.1	6.1	3.3	111.5	3.2	7.2
CEDEAC	*4. Central Africa*	19.2	1534	550	4.9	6.9	2.8	4.1	16.2	22.5	5.9	0.9	31.4	2.7	6.3
CEDEAC	*5. Great Lakes*	7.8	450	146	1.2	1.6	1.4	1.8	11.7	13.3	2.4	–3.1	65.6	2.8	6.3
COMESA	*6. Southern Africa (SADC)*	42.0	850	300	7.9	9.2	7.5	9.0	31.2	43	3.7	1.8	105	3.2	6.7
COMESA	*7. Indian Ocean*	8.1	1083	460	1.5	2.3	2.1	2.9	4.9	7.9	–	2.5	17.2	2.5	5
COMESA	*8. Eastern Africa*	34.8	771	155	2.0	3.8	4.6	7.1	15.2	43.2	–	3.8	158.4	3	7
COMESA	*9. South Africa*	125.9	4958	3310	23.6	18.1	18.3	26.8	18.3	25.6	4.1	1.3	41.0	2.4	4.3
	Total: Sub-Saharan Africa	**302**	**1214**	**490**	**61.4**	**67.6**	**50.6**	**72.4**	**174.4**	**247.1**	**4.2**	**2.5**	**645**	**2.8**	**6.5**
	Pacific East Asia	2377	–	890	217.0	371.0	224.0	395.0	221.7	477.2	7.3	6.0	1791	1.6	2.7
	South Asia	530	–	380	27.7	50.8	38.2	62.9	105.9	152.0	3.6	5.4	1326	2.2	4.2
	Middle East & North Africa	594	–	2710	112.6	–	89.9	–	–	212.0	6.7	2.9	302	3.1	5.7
	Latin America – Caribbean	1894	–	2200	123.2	261.0	101.1	315.6	422.3	656.4	6.0	3.6	515	2.1	3.3
	Total: World	**–**	**4622**	**4200**	**3187.9**	**5000.0**	**3355.7**	**5000.0**	**–**	**2095**	**4.0**	**3.1**	**5896**	**1.7**	**3.4**

1. *Burkina Faso, Cape Verde, Gambia, Mali, Mauritania, Niger, Senegal.*
2. *Benin, Ivory Coast, Ghana, Guinea, Guinea-Bissau, Liberia, São Tomé, Sierra Leone, Togo.*
4. *Cameroon, Congo, Gabon, Equatorial Guinea, Central Africa, Chad.*
5. *Burundi, Rwanda, Democratic Republic of Congo.*
6. *Angola, Botswana, Lesotho, Malawi, Mozambique, Swaziland, Tanzania, Zambia, Zimbabwe, Namibia.*
7. *Comoros, Madagascar, Mauritius, Seychelles.*
8. *Kenya, Uganda, Djibouti, Eritrea, Ethiopia, Somalia, Sudan.*

Sources: World Bank 1998; UNDP 1997; African Development Bank 2003. The GDP in US dollars is obtained by converting GDP in national currency at the official exchange rate. Merchandise exports and imports are expressed as FOB and CIF respectively. Total external debt is the sum of long-term public, publicly guaranteed and non-guaranteed private debt, recourse to IMF credit and short-term debt. Adjusted GDP uses purchasing power parity as a conversion factor.

PART ONE
THE MACROECONOMIC CRISIS

The wind blowing on Africa is no ordinary wind, it is a hurricane (Senghor).

There are no favourable winds for one who does not know where he is heading (Seneca).

From a macroeconomic perspective, Africa has experienced long-term stagnation of productivity in addition to external shocks that have induced serious instabilities: the loss of competitiveness has led to trade marginalisation. Africa has remained a "rent-orientated economy", where the process of accumulation has never really gotten under way.

In keeping with economic and financial relations, the *African economic crisis* has to be understood from the necessary, albeit reductionist, framework of macroeconomic coherence (World Bank 2000; Ravenhill 1988; Rose 1985). This crisis can be explained by the history of the *slave trade* (Chapter 1), while the exhaustion of resources caused by the practice of rent-orientated economics (Chapter 2) has led to its marginalisation vis-à-vis the centres of the world economy (Chapter 3).

Chapter 1
From the mercantilist era to the present crisis

A long-term historical perspective (Coquery-Vidrovitch 1989; Iliffe 1997) shows changes and continuities in man's relationship with his environment, in his self-portrayals, in his community, family and ethnic networks; that is, in the social relations and institutions at the heart of the course of change. Africa's pre-colonial, colonial and post-colonial past offers an in-depth explanation of the present crisis and how it differs from that of other continents.

1.1 From mercantilism to direct colonisation: 15th to the end of the 19th century

Triangular trade

During the "mercantilist" period, the direct colonisation of Africa remained limited (with the exception of the Cape Colony). Commercial penetration took place by setting up trading posts and ports of call as well as staging posts in the interior. In the countries of the savannah, large kingdoms were established on trade (the "empires" of Ghana and Mali, the Songhai, Mossi or Haoussa cities). The common term "empire" refers to the areas of expansion of ethnic groups rather than to the organisation of a political space controlled by an *imperium*. The Cape Colony (founded in 1652) was the largest European colony on the continent; it was, together with the east coast of Africa, an important refreshment station on the route to India. East Africa was not very accessible. Africa was dominated by the influence of Islam in the north, by Europe in the west, and by India and the Arab world in the east (Amselle & M'Bokolo 1985; Amin 1976; Ki Zerbo 1980; UNESCO 1980–1990).

Triangular trade linked Africa (supplier of slaves), the Americas (producer of precious metals and spices), and Western Europe. Control of this trade was at stake in major conflicts between European powers. The bulk of the trade took place between 1750 and 1860. Slavery (involving between 8 and 10 million men and women) remains very controversial. It considerably weakened the larger states in the African interior (e.g. Monomotapa and Congo), and favoured the small "broker" states: coastal peoples who were allies of the slave traders. It is agreed that these external relations left a deep imprint on Africa in producing a demographic vacuum and in modifying the spatial distribution of the population, notably by causing overpopulation in refugee areas, but also in destroying and transforming systems of production (most exporting and food-producing cultures came from the Indies).

The "inside" dynamics

The external reading given above is very reductionist. Internal histories give a different perspective. Since the ground-breaking work of Fortres and Evans Pritchard (1964), it has become acceptable to differentiate between *segmented societies* (societies composed of homogenous segments with a weak division of social labour) and *centralised systems*. This distinction is of importance only when one takes into account the complex combinations and the reversibility of trends. Thus, the Kingdom of Congo or the Mandingue "empire" of Mali become segmented societies.

Gatherer societies (for example, the pygmies of the equatorial forest or the Bushmen of southern Africa) had a *draining economy*. They had to face two contradictory demands: holding sway over a sufficiently large space to feed the population (it has been calculated that 260 hectares would have been necessary to support 10 people), and maintaining a sufficient population to ensure their own endogenous production.

In *segmented lineage societies without a state*, where agriculture was dominant, village communities provided the framework for control of the soil; membership could not be privately appropriated but was periodically allocated by the chief to members of the segments and sub-segments of the tribal lineage.[1] The circulation of

1 Lineage refers to people descending (in reality or fictively) from a common ancestor; production relations are formed around these ties to ensure reproduction of both the means of existence and of the people. The power of the elders thus rests upon their control of the means of human reproduction: victuals and women, and on prestige goods. The rules of accumulation are narrowly linked to the organisation of ceremonial relationships.

goods operated in two ways: service from the young to the elders, and redistribution from the elders to the young. Economic action would have been in line with social structures rather than determining them. Gathering activities and food-production were generally separated. Agriculture was extensive, and, if one takes into account the techniques practised (burning and long fallowing of land), the maximum density was around 30 inhabitants per square kilometre. These societies were organised according to the *rules of kinship* (Balandier 1971; Meillassoux 1975; Rey 1971). The extended or poly-nuclear family constituted the matrix of the economic (gender division of labour), political (hierarchy according to age), and religious (cult of ancestors) systems.

"State" societies were based on centralised systems. The political organisation of the big "empires" of western Africa (Ghana in the 11th century, Mali in the 14th century, Songhai and Bornou at their peak in the 16th century) leant upon their trade with the Arab world. The networks of large traders assured long-distance trade, notably that in gold, kola nuts and slaves. The economic base of other "empires" rested more upon the payment of a tribute (the Wolof state in Senegal, the Haoussa in Nigeria, or the Merina in Madagascar from the 16th to the 18th century).

Pre-colonial economies

It is dangerous to try to link the above *pre-colonial economies* to violent events in the histories of the various peoples, as they are very diverse. One can but put forward the hypothesis that economic and technical vulnerability largely favoured the social cohesion of communities and a hierarchy of powers.

The environments of these economies were harsh and natural conditions were hostile (insects and parasites, endemic diseases, poor soil, climatic risks, and so forth). The technical levels of the hunter-gatherer economies corresponded to that of the Palaelithic Age, and for agricultural societies to the Neolithic age. The wheel, writing or ploughing with animals was unknown in Africa until the 19th century, with Ethiopia being a notable exception. The absence of infrastructure networks made it difficult to circulate goods (Giri 1986).

Most of the relevant societies were characterised by hierarchies based on age. In fact, elders had to play the role of mediator between the living and their ancestors: they guaranteed harmonious relations between the society and the world of visible and invisible forces and they protected the society against external threats, often with "simple totalitarianism" (Médard 1991). These communities did not engage in trade relations.

Thus, the historical development of African societies was a result of the interplay between international and internal factors. These societies cannot be reduced to images of communities without a history, simply maintaining themselves, but ignorant of money and innovation. Demographically, Africa has remained underpopulated and has, it seems, stagnated notwithstanding strong fluctuations in development.

However, African economies evolved significantly during the 19th century. The abolition of the slave trade; the progressive disappearance of the mercantilist system; the settling of missionaries and colonists; and, in some regions of Africa, the beginning of direct colonisation were all factors that progressively opened the way for direct colonisation at the end of the 19th century. In Mauritius, the enfranchisement of slaves in 1833 led to the immigration of Indians. In 1822, freed United States slaves founded Liberia, which became independent in 1847. Senegal became a French colony in the mid-19th century.

1.2 Direct colonisation (1870–1960)

The expression of an archaic form of capitalism

After 1870, the European powers divided the bulk of Africa among themselves. Direct colonisation took place through the transposition of a metropolitan *state apparatus*. The latter was to "pacify", to create a regulatory framework, and carry out basic economic functions. It nonetheless leaned on some existing institutions and cannot be analysed as a mere transposition of a foreign body.

Contrary to the claims of those historians who interpret this as the expansion of dominant capitalism, colonisation was rather the economic outcome of the collapse of some European nations, protecting obsolete firms faced with international competition. As an expression of archaic capitalism, the "slave economy" relied on altered foreign structures and "indigenous" structures with regard to the role of the administration and trading societies (Pourcet 1979).

Merchant capital appreciated at the expense of productive capital. The colonial system was focussed more on withdrawal and reserving than on adding value and accumulation.

Whatever the case, the colonial reality was far removed from the triumphalist vision of military and political leaders looking to finance their conquests (Berry 1985). Investors noted that there was no labour market and that there was even a shortage of labour ("laziness and indolence of the indigenous people"); markets were minuscule; insecurity abounded (illness, climate); and communication means were almost non-existent. Thus, in order to achieve its objectives, the colonial state apparatus had to create everything; therefore the principle of self-financing was very quickly (1901) adopted for the French colonies.

Once assured of order, one of the priorities was to create infrastructure, i.e. "to colonise is to transport". Since foreign financing was inadequate, these public works were realised through labour-intensive procedures at a very high human cost (see for example the construction of the Congo-Atlantic Ocean railway).

The mobilisation of a surplus (the difference between production and the portion necessary to reconstitute the conditions of production) was ensured through compulsory measures (taxes, forced labour, obligatory cultivation and the expropriation of land). Investments were limited, except at the beginning of the period and in the wake of the Second World War (Marseille 1984; Suret-Canale 1977). Given the conquests, repression, forced labour and conscription, the African *population* did not grow much until the 1930s: estimated at 100 million at the end of the 19th century, it reached 150 million in 1950.

The colonial system

The *colonial system* was characterised by four main facets (Hugon 1968; Grellet 1982). The first was the setting up of an *administration*. The commercial apparatus by itself was incapable of breaking the pre-colonial framework and controlling the population. The political administrative systems certainly differed according to the colonisers: British *indirect rule* can be distinguished from the French *direct administration* and "assimilation". The French adapted their approach according to existing systems and resistance. In "state-like" societies, such as Madagascar, the existing state apparatus served as the basis of the colonial administration; in the Sahel regions military forts were used to maintain control.

The second big colonial concern was that of *ownership of the land*. In fact, with a few exceptions, territory under communal control was not transferable. Several systems were tried out: the large concessions of central Africa; direct colonisation; small-scale indigenous exploitation; and the Wakefield system (the sale of land at inflated prices to finance immigration and create a wage-earning class). Only in some countries (Kenya, Zimbabwe, Zambia, Madagascar and South Africa) did the colonisers appropriate land and this covered only five per cent of arable land. The capitalist mining economy was limited to areas such as South Africa, Zambia's Copperbelt, and the Katanga mines.

The *domination of merchant capital* was the third characteristic of colonisation. Property taxes, the monetisation of the dowry, and the

FIGURE 1: FLOWS WITHIN THE COLONIAL TRADE ECONOMY

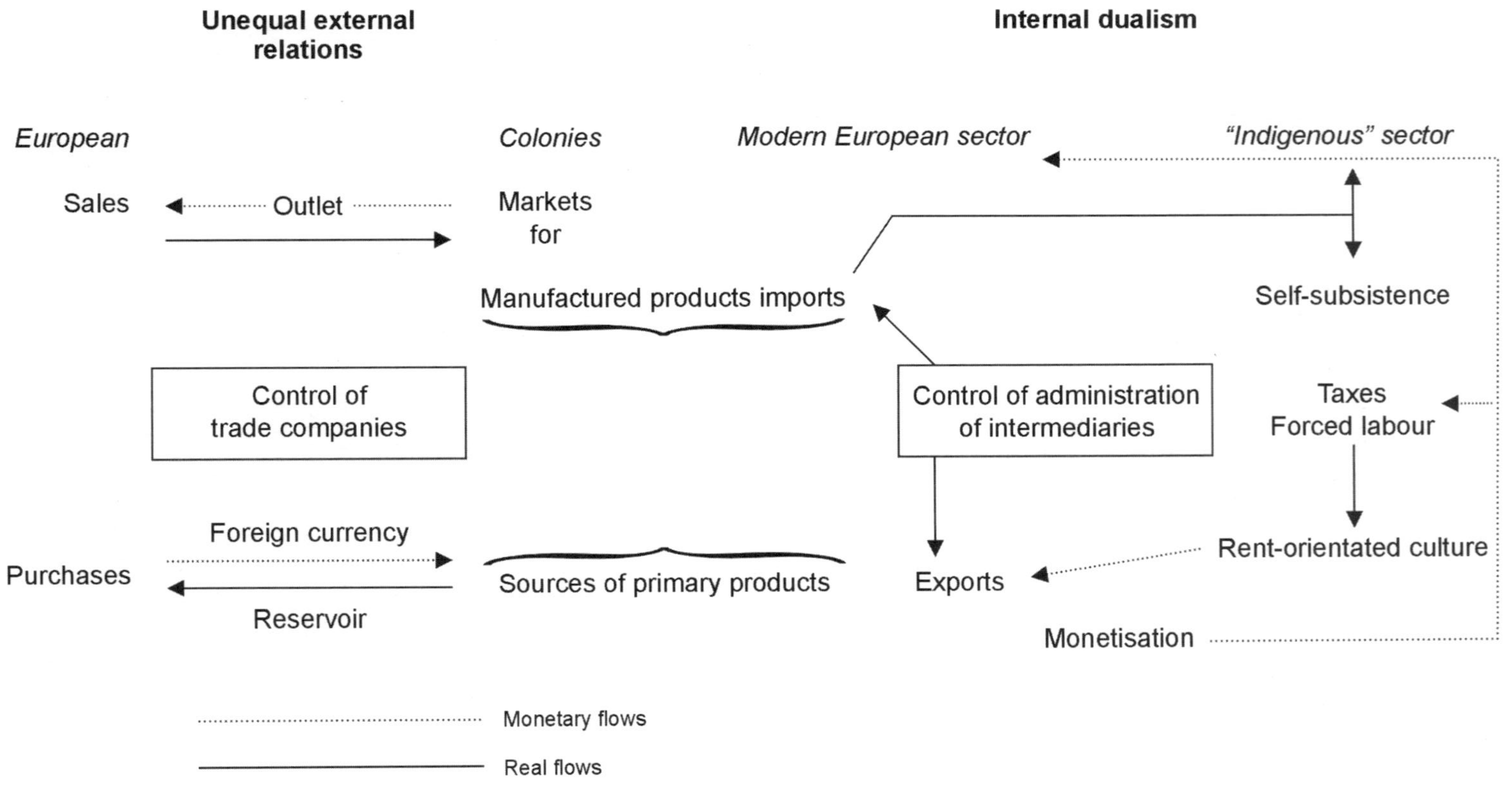

obligation to grow export crops were the means used as much to generalise the merchant economy as to develop agricultural production. Trading companies played a central role: the mother company generally had a centralised factory and subsidiaries or *bush factories*. These companies held the monopoly on external trade. More than the imperial monopoly, the method of monetisation provided the medium for market capture. The currency distributed through the buying of agricultural products was recuperated when *captive* trading firms sold consumer goods (Assidon 1989). The logic of *unequal trade* led to low prices. From the 1920s onwards, and especially since the 1929 crisis, the state provided the monetary function: it priced exports 20 per cent above world prices, while trading companies turned to import activities.

Finally, the privileged relations between the European metropolis and its colonies partly reproduced the former *colonial pact* (monopoly of the flag, polarisation of the flows between colony and metropolis, protection of colonial markets, overpriced imports and exports). The new pact was realised by the bias towards import-export companies in relation to freight companies and banks (Capet 1958; Bauer & Yamey 1968). The model of the *colonial trade economy* ("économie de traite") could be schematised in this way.

The colonies were reservoirs for exotic products and outlets for certain manufactured products. Corresponding to this external trade, controlled by monopoly companies, was the internal dualism between the European sector (modern) and the indigenous sector (traditional). The former represented the bulk of the added value and of the market (in 1960 the 40 000 Europeans in Madagascar represented more than 50 per cent of the local market). The two sectors were linked by foreign intermediaries (Greek-Lebanese in West Africa; Indians and Chinese in East Africa and the Indian Ocean). The administration forced the establishment of a *rent*-orientated culture. The agents of the modern sector imported what they consumed and exported what the peasants produced. These weakly linked sectors did not allow for progressive internal productivity.

It seems impossible to give an objective economic assessment of colonisation. Colonisation took place during a brief period set against a long history. It certainly left an imprint on African societies, and the latter largely reinterpreted and appropriated the colonial contribution. Important progress was made in exporting crops, in infrastructure, and in social investments, albeit at a very high human cost. However, in a final analysis it is clear that, with rare exceptions, no sustainable dynamics were set in motion that could lead to progress in productivity.

Contrasting colonial models

One has to guard against referring to the stereotypical French cultural assimilation model, the Belgian utilitarian model, the Portuguese integrationist model, and the British commercial and indirect rule model, since colonial practices were linked to local structures. Nevertheless, certain characteristic traits do allow one to identify different colonial imprints.

Indirect rule dominated in the British colonies, advocated by Lugard in Nigeria; the French model was based on *direct administration* and therefore centralisation with weak administrative devolvement to the local level, where chiefdoms carried less weight. After the 1929 crisis, this practice was replaced by the principle of assimilation. The francophone countries inherited French administrative practices: centralisation, hierarchy, remuneration unrelated to productivity, rank according to qualifications, the seniority game, and so on. They followed the principle of free public services (for example, schooling and health care). This *Colbertian* model explains the present-day existence of such administrations and political regimes.

The colonial educational systems and cultural models differed. In the *British colonies*, local particularities were more respected: education was "adapted to the environment", private effort was accorded greater importance, and vernacular languages and professional training were encouraged. In the *Belgian colonies*, a very selective education was practised, in the vernacular language and linked to agricultural skills. The model followed in the *French territories* favoured a general education and a cultural French model, and allowed pupils to go into tertiary employment (office employees, interpreters, nurses, or teachers). The dualist system differentiated between "indigenous" education (BECP level) and that intended for French citizens. The relevant models had an undeniable impact on the appearance of national elites. On the other hand, the Portuguese "overseas provinces" differentiated between the educated *assimilados* and the non-assimilated population. ❒

An evolving system

Beyond the general characteristics discussed, the colonial economy experienced several phases.

"Pacification" by the military force was followed by the setting up of the administration. After the 1929 crisis, one notices the withdrawal of the mother countries from their empires, and the new policies that were implemented were viewed as "developmental" (e.g. the Sarrault Plan in French Africa). In the face of a fall in the prices of primary goods, overpricing and protectionist measures were put in place, turning Africa into an inflated price location. Rural training operations, linked to progress in research and communication routes, led to productivity gains in agriculture. This raised a debate between the proponents of "assimilation" and those of "adaptation" of the indigenous population. This system was profoundly transformed in the wake of the Second World War due to public aid (for example, the FIDES Plan). Public investment in economic and social infrastructure had a crowding in effect on private investment (Maldant 1973). Positive public transfers (of funds to the African states) were compensated for by private sector export flows.

One notes a general onset of rural development operations, the beginning of import substitution industries and the valorisation of primary products, and, on average, a higher economic annual growth rate (five to six per cent). There is the unlocking of demographic expansion, a migration towards cities and an educational explosion, as well as a reconversion of commercial capital into industrial capital thanks to incentives and protective measures, and the development of *state capitalism* supported by external aid. Finally, there is an intensification of prospecting and mining exploitation.

Protective dispositions and stabilising mechanisms were created (marketing boards). The state became the principal developmental agent and demands for assistance, which grass-roots communities could not assume, were transferred to the state, the bulk of its income coming from external trade. Assimilation policies in the French colonies led to unified education (the 1966 Deferre law for French possessions), payment of public salaries without any link to average productivity (Lamine Gueye law), and the establishment of a labour code. The model adopted by the French foreign ministry, the central office for economic co-operation or the National School of Administration was that of a managed economy, of protected factory costs, where the state played a central role and where *interventionism* was reconciled with the specificity of dualistic societies. Liberal thinking and management methods carried little weight, in contrast to the situation in some anglophone countries where there was greater reference to the market and to trade liberalisation ("trade not aid").

1.3 Independence (1960–2004)

The gradual decline of the post-colonial model

In the case of the former French and English colonies, the transformation was partly prolonged during the first decade of independence, while sub-Saharan Africa moved from bilateral to multilateral relations. With the exception of Nigeria, there had been a general dismantling of federations (for example, Equatorial French Africa and French West Africa).

Foreign capital remained dominant. Thus in 1970, in the francophone countries, 70 per cent of the cumulated social capital of processing industries belonged to foreigners. The post-colonial state, in conflict and in competition with foreign firms, took over the colonial administration with government officials gradually forming those classes that monopolised both external and internal rents (Terray 1987; Bayart 1989).

As in the former British colonies, the state, in the absence of private role-players and in view of the rudimentary nature of the market, was supposed to allow for the change from a subsistence economy to a modern economy. It controlled the bulk of investments, regulated the economy through an *administered price* system and put in place the instruments of Keynesian macroeconomic policy. Some people's democracies (Mozambique, Ethiopia) in terms of Leninism, established a bureaucratic system mostly financed by foreign mining enclaves (Angola, Guinea). On the political front, almost all countries (Senegal was an exception) adopted the one-party system (military dictatorships, Islamic republics of Mauritania and the Comoros). The dynamics of most of these depended on primary product exports and external aid. Overpricing was replaced by aid for diversification and by guaranteed prices in the framework of their agreements with the European Economic Community (now known as the European Union). With the exception of the franc zone and the rand zone, monetary areas disappeared with independence.

The post-colonial model was gradually coming to an end: in one sense, the economy of indebtedness of the 1970s slowed down the crisis, though it would intensify in the future. Under external pressure from bankers and merchants in developed countries, and wishing to reclaim some of the economic power, national decision makers put in place unsuitable projects called "white elephants" and nationalised foreign financial enterprises primarily through taking external loans. The statist model of *industrialisation* was characterised by over-investment; an absence of any linkages to the local economy; and weak external competitiveness. Agricultural exports grew more slowly than imports. The process of *import substitution* became costly. Public and parastatal expenditures rose as a result of growing recourse to the state and diversions from its main functions.

At the beginning of the 1980s, the slowing down of the world economy affected these fragile economies, characterised by both budget and current account deficits. Beyond their objective of bringing about macroeconomic stability, *structural adjustment policies were aimed at transforming administered rent-orientated economies into market economies.*

Africa remains confronted with several problems that have existed since independence (an almost exclusive dependence on the export of primary products; the absence of an industrial base; weak savings and investment levels; limited profit-earning capacity of capital; limited coverage of health and educational needs), while having to manage public debt arrears and respond to demographic challenges. The establishment of many of the African states, in reality still in the process of being formed, has preceded the concept of a nation. Citizenship is an embryonic idea. Associated organisations within communities (tontines, associations, NGOs) and membership of smaller groupings within the community related to ethnicity, lineage, and so on, remain the dominant references of identity.

Public matters are dealt with through practices that are often exploitative and bureaucratic. "Benevolent" authoritarian regimes, the guardians of public well-being, have often been handed over to bureaucratic or predatory regimes and thus have partly justified a type of "rent-seeking" approach.

Nevertheless, African economies are undergoing a profound institutional transformation. The overburdened state can no longer undertake its former functions with regard to the needs of its constituents, that is, the maintenance of institutional structures endowed with certain powers; central decision-making organs; negotiating and compromising authority; and the production of goods and services. Institutional reforms have aimed to create a legal entity guaranteeing contracts, favouring property rights and enabling good governance. Privatisation has led to the state's disengagement from the productive sphere. Sovereignty has been transferred to sub-national (through decentralisation) and supranational (role of the Bretton Woods institutions) levels. Associations, NGOs, cooperatives, and the informal economy are playing an ever-increasing role as the producers of collective goods and services. Nevertheless, this has resulted not as much in the establishment of a market economy, but rather in the reconstruction of "rent-seeking" economies, as much in their external relations as in their internal functioning.

Chapter 2
Rent-orientated economy

A historical overview is essential in order to understand the present peculiarities of the African economies. Consideration of the legacies left by the central role of the community, the large trade networks of pre-colonial empires and colonial offices specialising in exotic cultures, is essential in understanding the present structure of the rent-orientated economy.

Many econometric studies explain the weak African performance (Collier & Gunning 1999; Sachs & Wagner 1997; Arcand & Guillaumont 2000). A number of contributing factors have been presented: *ethnic-linguistic fragmentation* (Easterly & Levine 1995); *geographical issues* (distance from coasts, poor quality of soil, illness, etc.) (Bloom & Sachs 1998); *historical issues* (poor specialisation, the role of colonialism); *political factors* (authoritarianism creating transaction costs, corruption in particular); *infrastructural factors* (weak telecommunications, lack of electricity, transport and public services); *international factors* (exposure to external shocks affecting their specialisation in primary products and the small size of the African economies).

Despite significant internal transformation, with rare exceptions, the African economies continue to be dominated by the *plantation economy* and/or the *mining economy.* A sectional division indicates an absence of linkages between the means of production (imported) and the means of consumption (imported or supplied by the domestic or informal sectors). These economies have a tendency to stagnate, with strong fluctuations linked to the valuation of rent; they are characterised by resource wastage, weak linkages between labour remuneration and factor productivity, and distortions between production and consumption methods. The bulk of *surplus* capital (or rent), originating from the primary sector and external aid, is converted into the importation of goods and services with hardly any spillover into productive activities. This rent is largely monopolised by those who are members of the state bureaucracy, who distribute it through clientilistic networks, or move it outside of the country in their private capacity. African "elites" have inherited a Western model (a strong propensity for the consumption of imported products), which is incompatible with what is possible under conditions of average production (Amin 1976).

2.1 Stalled accumulation

Economic stagnation

There are several factors that explain the *stagnation of accumulation*: the low rate of capital-intensive investment; distortions favouring non-productive sectors; weak demand; and a shortage of foreign currency for the importation of capital goods. Import substitution has failed to initiate a process of self-reliance leading to the diversification of production. Only a few countries, notably Mauritius, Botswana and South Africa, have escaped these impoverishing circumstances.

Having exceeded demographic growth between 1961 and 1973 (4,6 per cent), real GDP growth for the African states fell to 2,1 per cent between 1980 and 2000, and to 2,5 per cent between 1990 and 2000. During the second half of the 1990s, economic growth picked up again. In 1999 and 2000, overall GNP growth was 2,2 per cent, but around one per cent in Nigeria and South Africa, half the world average.

In the short term, GDP growth is dependent upon import capacity, itself a function of the volume exported, and the terms of any trade grants. Imports of intermediary and capital goods are complementary to production. In the long term, GDP growth depends on production capacity, itself a function of production factors and their productivity growth. In the Ivory Coast, a growth of one per cent in EDI led to a rise of 3,1 per cent in production capacity, and one per cent investment growth led to a two per cent growth in production capacity (Hugon in Tapinos et al. 2001).

Whereas one can see a relationship between savings and investment in developing countries (indicating the weak international mobility of capital), this relationship is weak or absent in African countries. On the one hand, investment is a function of external finance. On the other, there is no significant correlation between savings, investment, and growth. The propensity to marginal savings is almost the same as in other countries: an increased income

TABLE 2: GDP GROWTH IN SUB-SAHARAN AFRICA (%)

	1961–1973	*1973–1980*	*1980–1990*	*1990–2000*	*2000–2003**
Annual population growth rate	2,6	2,8	3,1	2,6	2,5
Annual GDP growth rate (a)	4,6	2,7	2,1	2,5	3,0
Gross investment rate as a % of GDP (b) I	15,0	20,6	6,0	6,0	8,0
Marginal capital output ratio (b)/(a)	3,3	7,6	7,6	6,5	6,0
End of period GDP structure (%)	100	100	100	100	100
Private consumption C_p	72	66	68	69	N/A
Public consumption C_g	11	13	15	16	N/A
Exports X	22	26	29	28	N/A
Imports M	19	25	28	30	N/A
Gross domestic savings S	14	22	16	15	N/A

Or: S_i gross domestic savings; S_e external savings; S_p private savings, S_g public savings; S_n gross national savings; X exports of non-factor goods and services; M imports of non-factor goods and services; T_i net transfers; R_f net factor income; Y_d private sector disposable income; C_p private sector consumption; T government income; C_g public consumption; Y GNP; I investment (I_g public investment and I_p private investment)

$$S_i = (Y_d - C_p) + (T - C_g) = I_g + I_p$$

$$Y - (C_p + C_g) + [(M - X) - R_f - T_r] = 1$$

Or: s_i domestic savings rate S/Y; i the investment rate I/Y; s_e the external savings rate $(X - M + R_f + T_r)/Y$; gy the GDP growth rate dY/Y; c the marginal capital output ratio. The growth model is written as:

$$gy.c = i = (s_i + s_e)$$

Sources: World Bank Statistics 1991; African Development Bank 2000.

* Author's projections.

gives rise to a high savings rate growth, but the African countries are at a lower per capita income threshold. Thus the gap between savings and investment is filled by external financing, leaving these countries caught in the "debt trap": low income and low growth hamper internal resource mobilisation and lead to external financing; and inefficient and costly investments slow down growth. Financing is mainly public; private financing is limited due to low anticipated growth, and risks are subject to the vulnerability of human resources and fluctuations in public capital.

Convergence tests show that Africa differs from the rest of the world. Most African economies have not reached the threshold in the accumulation of production factors and public capital to allow them to overcome the poverty trap.

Slow accumulation rate

Economic stagnation in sub-Saharan Africa can be explained by the weak *investment rate* and especially by *bad investment*. During the period 1975 to 1988 (World Bank 1991), one can detect a significant correlation between the rate of private and public investment and the GNP growth rate, indicating the negative effect of debt and the inflation rate on investment; and also indicating the negative effect, albeit to a lesser degree, of appreciation of the real exchange rate and, on the other hand, the seemingly neutral role played by inflation and exchange rate instability.

The effect of under capitalisation on the low economic growth in Africa is much debated. Most studies put forward macro- and microeconomic factors to explain a low investment rate and even, in the end, limited growth. In contrast, some research (Devarajan, Easterley, Pack 2001) has tested the low productivity of especially public investment, whereas Hussain (2000) mentions the low productivity of investment in trade terms for countries experiencing foreign currency constraints.

The share of investment in the GDP dropped from 20 per cent during the 1970s to 15 per cent in later decades. The savings rate also dropped. This fall took place in countries from all the different categories, with the exception of the oil-producing countries that experienced a fall in their savings rate only during the second half of the 1980s. Investments were increasingly financed externally (43,4 per cent on average and 60,5 per cent in the low-income countries).

Moreover, the confidence crisis and the *increase in risks* led to a fall in the marginal productivity of capital in the face of real interest rates, which generally became positive. The marginal capital output ratio, measuring 3,2 between 1960 and 1970, rose to 7,6 between 1970 and 1980 and between 1980 and 1990; whereas in Southeast Asia, during the same period, it was 4,2; 5,0 and 5,2 respectively. There are several explanations for this. Investments were primarily orientated towards indirect productive infrastructure. During the 1970s, external finance was used mainly to pay for the wasteful "white elephants" (Adjaokuta in Nigeria, Inga in former Zaire). In the context of the recession of the 1980s, maintaining public and especially private consumption led to a fall in investment. During the adjustment period, there was a drop in investment and no significant increase in savings. Financing remained esentially public. Private financing remained limited, in spite of privatisation, due to numerous factors, such as weak anticipated growth, risks inherent to shock vulnerability and weakness of public and personal capital. The economic development indicator (EDI) only represents one per cent of the global total and one notes weak reinvestment of this share, despite an estimated profitability of 28 per cent in petroleum investments and in niche markets. One estimates that 40 per cent of African savings are reinvested in financial markets outside of Africa. These different factors all reflect the *malfunctioning of financial systems.*

2.2 Financial malfunctioning

The financial system plays a very important role in economic development (transformation of liquid assets into non-liquid assets, mutualisation and transformation of individual risk, and the mobilisation of savings and credit). The credit market revolves around intermediate transactions where confidence and proximity come into play. With the exception of South Africa, the financial systems of African states are not greatly diversified. Intermediary financial costs are high. Financial markets are very basic. Only in South Africa does the JSE stock market capitalisation exceed the GDP.

Financial dualism

Financial circuits are segmented: there is external private financing among branches of multinational corporations, external public financing through aid, internal public state financing, internal private banking financing, and financing through informal and usury channels. The *institutional financial system* (central bank, development banks and commercial banks) takes care only of the modern sector; it tends to favour short-term financing linked to commercial or speculative activities, or credit to the private sector. Decentralised financing (mostly limited) serves the majority of the population that does not qualify for formal banking. It is characterised by flexible organisation, is socially anchored and has a low cost. The *informal financier* plays the important role of financial intermediary; in some regions (for example the Bamileke region in Cameroon) it is as big as the formal banking sector and plays the same role. It certainly plays a bridging role, especially in financing the informal productive sector, but it is generally still driven by a short-term logic; it will be with difficulty that these informal financial institutions transform into genuine credit institutions. Many needs are not covered by these financial systems, such as housing, agricultural-, handcraft- and industrial projects, as well as Small and Medium Enterprise (SME) investments.

Financial dualism increased during the 1970s: the indebtedness of the *treasury* to the central bank, the high deficits of public enterprises and their priority access to credit caused financing to be redirected at the expense of the private sector. Banks accumulated *bad debts* that were difficult to recover.

The *1980s and 1990s* were marked by a major reorganisation linked to financial liberalisation. Nevertheless, in the context of management costs, provincial networks were closed down and there was a reorientation towards external operations that were more profitable in the short term (rural credit and import-export financing). Consequently, the increase in *external debt* was evidence of the accumulation of internal debt by companies as well as the state. Overlapping debts and general indebtedness contributed to the serious disruption of the financial system. Micro-finance began to expand.

The *financial repression* theory, which stresses negative real interest rates and selective credit policies, has some validity. Nevertheless, institutional factors can explain why the replacement of private investment by public investment prevails over the effects of dispossession, or why the real interest rate hardly impacts on the savings level, even if it has an effect on the structure of savings and the efficiency of investments. The impact of financial liberalisation, however, is limited owing to the "poverty trap".

Public deficits

Consolidated budget and public enterprise deficits largely explain financial dysfunction. At the time of independence, new states had to face the *high expenditures* of sovereignty: they had to embrace development while also ensuring the satisfaction of basic social needs (education and health). International instability also furthered the *impoverishing effects*. During high-income periods governments launched investment projects that generated recurrent costs and recruited large workforces, which created a *standstill* in public expenditure. The administrative machinery gradually got into financial deep water (Severino & Servant 1992).

Development indicators

Economic statistics are hardly reliable. Economists should be careful when considering the expansion of formerly unquantified sectors in relation to the sophistication of recent economics. For example, the incorporation of informal economic activities has doubled the GDP of the former Zaire (now Democratic Republic of the Congo).

However, economic growth, measured by the GDP, differs from economic development, which is defined as an endogenous and cumulative process leading to an increase in productivity and a reduction of inequalities in the long term, thus allowing a growing number of inhabitants to move out of a situation of insecurity and vulnerability to a situation where they can manage their insecurities and instabilities and satisfy their basic needs. Economic growth in the Ivory Coast, Cameroon, and Nigeria was more the result of increasing rent than of the dynamics of the productive system.

In 2000, there were 35 African countries among the 57 low-income countries (less than US$700 per capita) in the world. This indicator, however, is inadequate on several counts:

- *Heterogeneous prices and quantities (the problem of balancing)*. Depending on whether one uses the prices and exchange rates of 1980 or 1987, Nigeria represented 50 per cent or 20 per cent respectively of the GDP of sub-Saharan Africa, and the economy of the latter stagnated or grew by 15 per cent between 1980 and 1987.
- *Accounting unit bias*. Most comparisons are made in US dollars. The domestic buying power of a currency is higher than that indicated by the exchange rate. This gap varies inversely to the level of real per capita income. Thus, the per capita GDP gap (1998) between the United States and Ethiopia varies from US$292 to US$5 (taking account of purchasing power parity).
- *Non-merchandised goods and services*. National accounting captures only merchandised goods and

services, or those goods and services that can be sold on the market. This excludes domestic activities, environmental pollution and social costs (self-consuming activities are estimated at market prices). Many informal activities that would be considered domestic or public activities in industrialised countries are sold in African cities, but escape statistical registration.

According to the Human Development Report (2000) of the United Nations Development Programme (UNDP), the *human development indicator* (HDI) is an aggregate reflecting life expectancy at birth, literacy rates and the adjusted per capita GDP (that is, taking account of the purchasing power parity of different currencies). Five of the six poorest countries in the world are in Africa (Mali, Nigeria, Burkina Faso, Sierra Leone and Guinea), four of which are in the Sahel. The *human poverty indicator* (HPI) is associated with life expectancy, education, and basic services (health, clean water, and nutrition) deficits. Multidimensional poverty is expressed in terms of low monetary income, satisfaction of basic needs, disposal of assets, and weak social functioning. According to Sen it refers to insufficient "entitlements" and "capabilities".

In 2003, 34 of the 49 least-developed countries (LDCs) belonged to sub-Saharan Africa, that is, 350 million inhabitants out of 614 million. Three criteria are used to determine this category: a per capita GNP of less than US$900 (the average is US$287), a composite social indicator close to the human development indicator (HDI) (the average is 66 per cent illiterate inhabitants, 10 per cent without running water and 10 per cent mortalities before one year of age) and a composite social indicator (poor transformation of primary products, poor quality of manufactured goods ...). On the other hand, vulnerability, exterior influences and weak resilience are not included as criteria.

Inclusion in the category of LDCs allows access to certain advantages, such as the alleviation of debt (eg. Highly-Indebted Poor Countries), concessionary loans and commerce (the EU's "Everything but arms"-initiative). ❒

Tontines, decentralised financing and micro finance

During the Mazarin era, the banker Tonti developed survival tontines: the subscription of individuals to a joint fund eventually to be shared among the surviving subscribers.

In *informal* finance, the use of liquid funds, which involves the forging of personal relations, prevails over the banking circuit's invisible money, and one can distinguish between voluntary and forced savings associations (Dupuy & Servet 1987):

- Saving societies based on community solidarity are defined by the forced nature of the individual membership, and by a system of reciprocity and benefits or redistribution.
- On the contrary, the *tontine* ("stokvel" in South Africa), is based on voluntary individual membership. Relationships are built on a contractual basis. Membership is temporary and centres on the objective of saving and collective credit. One can distinguish three types of tontines (Lelart 1990):
  – The *mutual tontine* has rotating savings, where each member can collect money according to a pre-established, but revisable order.
  – The *commercial tontine* has a fixed savings fund, administered by a managing "money keeper" who receives contributions and consents to loans. The parties to this type of tontine thus fulfil certain

Besides its normal functions, the *state* regulated graduate unemployment and became a space of *rent appropriation*. Furthermore, in several countries at war, *military expenditure* represented a very large share of the GDP, rising from an average of 0,7 per cent to 3,2 per cent in 1969 and 1989 respectively. In some of the countries at war, it represented more than five per cent of the GDP (Angola, Rwanda, Sudan, Eritrea). In 1992, military expenditure in the former Zaire and Uganda was more than 10 times higher than health expenditure.

Social expenditure was relatively important, particularly because of demographic factors and the cost of educational and health serv-

banking functions. Claims and debts carry interest. Deposits are more or less regular and reimbursements can be provided before the foreseen date.
– In the *financial tontine* the levies collected are auctioned off in accordance with a financial intermediary. Interest payments collected on each loan are capitalised and taken into account.

Therefore, behind each type of tontine there is a very varied continuum, stretching from a social point of view related to community solidarity to a financial point of view based on utilitarian calculations. The involvement of the tontine group members increases the power of withdrawal for each individual: members do not want loans, but want funds to be available on a temporary basis, since uncertainty makes arbitration between an assumed financial risk and a received reward impossible. In an uncertain environment, where there is a strong preference for liquidity (especially to face the most urgent needs for survival), those who renounce immediate liquidity want to be able to recuperate their funds quickly and reduce the number of parties to the tontine when the need arises. Decentralised financing systems (DFSs) (grass-roots banks, financial societies, savings and cooperative credit networks, mutual credit, joint credit) limit the negative selection phenomenon of the official systems and finance those excluded from these systems (Gentil & Hugon 1996). ❒

ices. Public expenditure on education and health represented 4,1 per cent and one per cent respectively of the GDP in 1990. These social expenditures tended to fall during the 1980s and 1990s.

On average, *wage expenditure* represented more than 40 per cent of state expenditures and often reached 70 to 80 per cent. From the colonial period, African countries inherited high salary levels in relation to the per capita income. At the time of independence, a teacher earned almost 30 times more than the average per capita income. Since then there has been a flattening of real salaries owing to a stagnation in nominal salaries and inflation, and in 2000, a teacher

TABLE 3: MACROECONOMIC AND INVESTMENT INDICATORS IN SUB-SAHARAN AFRICA (%)

					Indicators		
	Investment rate	Private investment rate	Public investment rate	Debt/ GDP	Real exchange rate 1980 = 100	Inflation instability	Real exchange rate instability
1975–1988	18,4	10,4	8,0	41,4	98,8	0,091	1,234
1975–1981	21,7	12,8	8,9	27,0	94,7	0,094	1,230
1982–1988	15,4	8,1	7,3	55,8	102,9	0,089	1,226
1991–2002	18	11,7	6,3	80	–	–	–

Sources: World Bank 1998, p. 129; African Development Bank 2003.

Contrasting monetary management

There is a mosaic of exchange and monetary regimes in Africa, which precludes a general overview.

The 15 countries of the franc zone, where currencies are converted and fixed against the franc, practise a rigorous *monetarist* policy. Since 1980, there has been a slowdown in the distribution of credit (prerequisite authorisation, refinancing ceilings). The ratio of money supply to the GDP has dropped. These countries saw their inflation rates come close to zero before the 1994 devaluation and there was a reduction in the debts owed by their treasuries to the central banks. Positive real interest rates favoured daily deposits. On the other hand, near money (account ledgers) was very limited.

In contrast, in some countries outside the franc zone inflation reached the same levels as those known in South America (in the case of former Zaire before 1997, Sierra Leone and Somalia). Annual growth rates of ready money and of inflation exceeded 50 per cent during the 1980s. Between 2000 and 2003, ten countries experienced inflation of at least a double figure (e.g. Angola and the DRC). The main sources of money creation were the government deficit and the anticipation of inflation by economic agents. Cumulative inflation furthered a freeze in supply and speculative investments. Dollarisation also lead to a double monetary circuit. ❐

earned almost seven times the average per capita income. Added to these costs were those implicit in the bureaucratic approach and exceptional discretionary power of the state ("everything is forbidden but can be bought"), leading to inefficiencies in allocations and productivity. One notes, since then, an adjustment from the bottom level, with a strong decline in salary expenditure and public investment, the increasing weight of public debt and a weak increase in revenue.

Public expenditure rose to more than 20 per cent of the GNP in 2002 (as opposed to 19 per cent in non-African low-income coun-

TABLE 4: PUBLIC FINANCE SITUATION (IN % OF GDP), AVERAGE 1987–1990

	Public withholding rate, i.e. taxes	*Current public expenditure rate*	*Public savings rate*	*Conventional deficit*
Franc zone	16,4	15,7	–3,1	–5,9
Outside franc zone, sample of 16 countries	19,0	19,0	–0,03	–6,5
Developing countries	17,3	20,2	–2,9	–6,5
Middle-income countries	22,8	26,0	–3,2	–9,7
Under adjustment	16,9	17,4	–0,5	–5,9
Without adjustment	23,4	23,4	–2,0	–6,5

Note: The rate of public withholding represents the percentage of revenue (apart from grants) to the GNP. The conventional deficit is equal to the difference between total public withholding (plus grants) and the entire public expenditure (apart from debt payments); it corresponds to the state's need for loans. The public savings rate is the difference between total public withholding and current expenditure (including interest on public debt).

Source: Severino & Servant 1992.

tries): current expenditure represented 17 per cent and capital expenditure, eight per cent of GNP. Subsidies and transfers amounted to more than three per cent of GDP. *Public debt* became an essential entry. During the *structural adjustment* era, the fall in public expenditure mainly affected investment expenditure and functional expenditure. Public debt exploded. Salaries decreased faster than the number of state employees.

Along with the pressures on expenditure, fiscal appropriation began to be eroded and public income to dry up. This in turn affected external trade relations (duties levied on imports and exports, royalties, and indirect taxes on imports). The reforms that were being put in place aimed to increase taxes on internal production and enlarge the fiscal basket. Tax evasion was widespread.

Revenue from internal added value (for example VAT and income tax) suffered from the effects of the slowing down of the GDP. Some economic activities took place outside the state's control and therefore escaped the internal revenue office. The erosion of the productive base of the formal sector led to a concentration of levies on some enterprises. An average of 20 per cent of the GDP was comprised of public levies (averages for 1979–1988): these rates were respectively 19,6 per cent in the franc zone and 15,6 per cent outside the franc zone. These rates (percentages of the following compared to the GDP of state income: fiscal, non-fiscal, surplus of state marketing boards, from equalisation and from state insurance) dropped during the 1980s. Down from 22,1 per cent in 1980–1981, they were 20,4 per cent in 1986–1987 and 16,5 per cent in 1987–1990. One nevertheless notes some increase in revenue and levies at the level of local finances.

During the structural adjustment period, the *primary budget surplus* (budget deficit minus interest on debt), which expresses the state's capacity to finance recurring costs and its own investments, improved, but in a regressive context of lowering revenue and expenditures, often preventing the state from fulfilling its statutory functions. In 1999, the budget deficit represented 2,9 per cent of African GDP. The global deficit of public finance has grown, as percentage of the GDP, from –6,3 (average 1980–1990) to –3,7 (1991–2002) (BAD, 2003).

Between 2000–2003, the budget balance/GDP varied considerably, according to the different regions: +4 per cent in oil-producing Central Africa, –4 per cent in eastern Africa, –3 per cent in southern Africa and relatively unchanged in western Africa.

TABLE 5: VALUE ADDED BY ASSETS IN SSA (EXCLUDING SOUTH AFRICA)

	Primary		*Secondary*		*Tertiary*	
	1965	1998	1965	1998	1965	1998
1) % Value added	40	19	20	30	40	52
2) % Working population	79	70	8	7,5	13	22,5
3) Value added per worker (1/2)	0,5	0,27	2,5	4,0	3,0	2,3

Source: UNDP 2000.

2.3 Sectoral imbalances

These financial imbalances reflect and emphasise a *stagnation in the productive system*. There were weak attempts to promote Keynesian multipliers (through income transactions), limited inter-industry trade, of which a large component consisted of imported inputs, and significant bottlenecks. The gap between agricultural and industrial added value rose from 5,0 in 1965 to 14,8 in 1998, and from 6,0 in 1965 to 8,5 in 1998 between agricultural and services added value. One can thus observe a decrease in primary sector added value.

Extensive food-producing agriculture

African food-producing agriculture remains traditional; it consumes few inputs, but a lot of space and is only in rare instances based on the ability to control water supply. Its dynamics are linked to the existence of urban markets that enable the selling of surplus produce. Of an *extensive* nature, it is hardly able to control risks (ploughing with animals and bush burning are practised). Cultivation for own consumption is prevalent. Backward and forward linkages to the rest of the economy have hardly been developed (Badouin 1979; Bates & Lofchie 1980; Couty et al. 1983; Lele 1989). "Intensive agriculture foods and extensive agriculture yields" (Pelissier 1966) as long as space and resources are managed as "free goods", that is, at no cost. The different natural heritages lead to a plurality of rights, concerning, for example, the hereditary conveyance of property and cultures. These tend to change due to the pressures of ownership and private property rights, something that gives security to owners, but is also a source of conflict. For 30 years the increase in agricultural production, with rare exceptions, came about through the extension of acreage and not through an improvement in yields. Intensive agriculture modernised through the use of irrigation, the double annual harvest, manure, use of high-yielding seeds and plants are found only in some areas (e.g. the Bamileke Plateaus in Cameroon, and South Africa).

There seems to be an "urban bias" (Lipton, 1977). To feed the cities, public marketing agencies (e.g. ONCAD in Senegal) have become massive bureaucracies. Thus, faced with controlled prices fixed at low levels, parallel markets have developed with trade intermediaries being the main beneficiaries. The attraction of imports in an environment of low international prices and the overvaluation of currencies has led to a counter-protection of agriculture. Nevertheless, this shows that the "urban bias" theory is debatable. The most urbanised countries have the highest relative added value and producer prices (Hugon et al. 1989). Cereal imports and food aid have doubled between 1974 (5 million tonnes) and 1980 (10 million tonnes). This stabilised between 1980 and 1995. In 2000, imports and aid reached 16 million tonnes. Food imports have been rising for 30 years, to about 15 per cent of total imports. Urban markets stimulate especially peri-urban food production (Cour 1992). Contrary to current thinking, Africa in general does not suffer from insufficient food production. It certainly suffers from price fluctuations, but production meets demand. Most food shortages are the result either of the absence of rights for certain groups, or of difficulties in accessing food as a result of violent conflicts.

The export agriculture crisis

The agricultural crisis is mainly that of *cultivation for export*. This grew at a high rate during the colonial era due to favourable prices (stabilised overpricing); training structures (European capitalist farmers, large plantations with a workforce, incentives for or constraints on small producers); and marketing and price stabilisation agencies. These factors were mitigated when Africa began to face international competition. Price stabilisation funds were malfunctioning badly before they were dismantled.

With rare exceptions (peanuts in Senegal, green beans in Burkina Faso, and coffee from the east coast of Madagascar) the development of cultivation for export (through better training, use of fertiliser, complementary cultivation or rotation) has been replaced by food cultivation. Thus, the production of cotton provided an important channel for training in the Sahel (for 20 years annual production grew by seven per cent a year).

Agriculture is the main source of surplus, but more because of price differentials between producers and export prices than through heightened productivity increasing volumes for export. The African peasantry suffers, to various degrees, from a triple effect: dependency (fall in international agricultural prices), dislocation (higher marketing margins), and a drain on income. From 1960 to 1980 the internal terms of trade between agricultural and other products deteriorated, and this acted as a disincentive (Faucher, in Guillaumont 1986). In Ghana, the Central Marketing Board employed 10 500 people in 1982, the cost of which appropriated half of the value added in the cocoa industry. During the 1970s, the overvaluation of the real exchange rate constituted an implicit tax on agricultural production. During the 1980s, in the context of depressed international prices, the depreciation of the real exchange rate led to a rise in the rate of public appropriation and marketing margins. Those countries that adopted incentive pricing (Ivory Coast, Kenya, Malawi) and/or stabilisation measures showed a remarkable increase in production. The factors causing a stagnation in agricultural production came down, in part, to *political distortions* and unfavourable prices.

Price stabilisation, guaranteed supply and the opening of markets played a determining role in increasing supply (compare the success of cotton in francophone Africa). Rural emigration; the low returns of public investments; marketing and supply difficulties; obsolete or unsuitable technologies; climatic (e.g. drought); ecological; social (lineage or land ownership structures); and political (e.g. war and insecurity) factors are *structural elements* that all had different impacts (Becker & Morrison 1990; Lipton 1977). There are certainly problems of production, but the root cause of the agricultural crisis can be located largely outside of agriculture: it is situated upstream (lack of fertiliser, seed, technique) and downstream (marketing, transport, stockpiling, secure outlets) of actual agricultural production. The consolidation of the cotton network in francophone Africa in the face of shortcomings and market transaction costs has enabled technical effectiveness and competitiveness in spite of cyclical financial deficits and the lack of transparency of the cotton companies.

Low agricultural productivity has had repercussions on the entire economy. Rent-orientated agriculture accounts for 30 per cent of export income in Africa: it is the main source of fiscal income for most states. Food production has to take account of feeding a population growing by more than three per cent a year and an urban population with a growth rate that varies between five and seven per cent. A technical revolution (cultivation by using animals to plough, intensification, a green revolution) is necessary.

De-industrialisation

African industrialisation has occurred only recently (De Bandt & Hugon 1988; Meier & Steel 1989). It took place in the wake of the Second World War, based on the increased value of resources and the substitution of imports for regional markets. Owing to protectionist measures, trading companies were encouraged to convert to industrial capital. These measures favoured industrial investment and caused it to grow by around eight per cent, twice the average rate of the economy, during the first decade of independence. During the 1970s, one saw the state taking over industrial investment (Ivory Coast, Ghana, Nigeria, Tanzania, and Zambia).

The unfavourable economic situation of the 1980s showed not only how frail the industrial system was, but simultaneously emphasised its importance; thus de-industrialisation occurred in the context of the reduction of protection, privatisation, liberalisation,

Industrial malfunctioning

Numerous factors contribute to industrial malfunctioning, four of which are discussed below:

- *The international environment* has been unstable and has been characterised by the rising power of new competitors and the increasing financial nature of international relations. In this regard, policies to lower protection and prevent smuggling have often led to a downgrading of the industrial apparatus. Since a large component of the production factors are paid for in foreign currency, exchange rate adjustments have not had the expected effects on international competitiveness. In the face of many risks, relative profitability is weak.
- *Macroeconomic factors* including the fall and magnitude of swings in the market (there is often a gap of 30 to 50 per cent between the swings in annual turnover) and the Balkanisation of markets. Many industries are constrained by the lack of demand. The institutional environment does not favour industrial enterprises. In some sectors there is strong competition from informal activities and

and a fall in demand. Industry hardly took off. The sector remained highly dependent on capital, technology, and labour. The industrial fabric was weak and there was a near absence of capital goods. The manufacturing sector contributed less than 10 per cent to the GDP (with the exception of South Africa); the one million people employed in manufacturing were three and a half times less than those working in industry in South Korea alone; exports, at less than US$2bn, were lower than those of Thailand; the share of sub-Saharan Africa (South Africa excluded) of global exports of manufactured products decreased from 0,5 per cent in 1980 to 0,3 per cent in 1990 (CEPII 1992).

Dualism is evident between the semi-artisan micro-businesses, managed in a traditional manner, and large public or private enterprises. Of the 345 industrial projects studied by the Enterprise Institute, 280 operated at a loss or far below their production capacity in 1986. Nevertheless, industrial infrastructures still exist in smuggling (e.g. second-hand clothes) (Géronimi, in Coussy & Hugon 1992).

- *Management and organisational problems.* Profit-making prevails over the creation of value; generally, over- and under-investment takes place, enterprises lack their own funds, and they have too much debt. Skills are under-utilised and salaries and productivity are not always linked. Social and political factors, indeed cultural factors, seem as important as economic factors.
- *Political economic choices.* African industry is often badly located, out of proportion, and technologically poorly managed. The *high actual protection* of industries (more than 50 per cent), negative real long-term interest rates, overvalued exchange rates, and regional policies point as much to voluntarist industrialisation conceived without taking into account criteria of profitability, efficiency and competitiveness. Socio-political rationality appears to have prevailed over financial and economic criteria. Bad economic location can be explained by criteria based on regional balance. Disproportionate size and under capitalisation are linked to financing methods and rents charged by decision makers. The duplication of industrial projects in regional economic groupings is a result of excesses. ❐

Zimbabwe, Mauritius, and Nigeria, and used to exist in Cameroon and the Ivory Coast. Five countries (Nigeria, Zimbabwe, Ivory Coast, Ghana, and Kenya) contribute 60 per cent of the manufacturing added value in sub-Saharan Africa. In South Africa alone, the industrial manpower equals that of the rest of sub-Saharan Africa (one million people).

The *mining and energy sector* makes up two-thirds of sub-Saharan Africa's exports, and plays an important role in some economies (Bomsel 1985; Giri 1986). Africa remains a surplus producer of energy. In 1995, Africa consumed 133,5 million tonnes of oil and oil-equivalents (of which 87 million tonnes was consumed in South Africa). In 2002, Africa produced 190 million tonnes of oil (of which Nigeria produced 104 and Angola 45 million tonnes). But forestry products in dry areas provide 90 per cent of its energy. Energy imports have risen from seven per cent to 28 per cent of merchandise exports between 1965 and 1990.

The heterogeneity of the tertiary sector

It is important to distinguish the several segments in this sector:

- The *intermediary tertiary sector* (allowing for the meeting of supply and demand) can be explained by the importance of transaction costs, trade, stockpiling and transport expenses in open economies broken up into sections that are not in contact with one another.
- The *luxury tertiary sector* stems from the unequal distribution of income and the payment of low wages (e.g. to domestic workers) or from the high rates charged for the rent of certain sites (e.g. tourist sites).
- The *survival tertiary sector* includes some so-called informal urban activities – from petty trade to pavement repair services and transport services.

Africa has remained a *mining environment* (30 per cent of global reserves). In the mid-20th century, there was an increase in the exploitation of mining resources: phosphates in Senegal and Togo, potassium in Congo, bauxite in Guinea, iron ore in Liberia and Mauritania, manganese and uranium in Gabon and chromium in Madagascar. Subsequently, apart from some successes (e.g. uranium in Niger), Africa's economic weight in the global mining economy has clearly declined and there has been a fall in the profitability of the *principal marginal mines*.

The crisis in the mining industry corresponded to a fall in commodity prices, which were often below production costs, and was exacerbated by competition on saturated global markets, while increased investment generated high external debts and created recurrent costs. In some cases, the decline of industries (e.g. the Copperbelt in Zambia or Gecamines in the former Zaire) led to a general economic downturn because of their pivotal role in the redistribution of economic activity, and this threatened the entire social and political fabric. With the exception of Botswana and South Africa, income from mining has hardly financed accumulation and has often been a factor leading to conflict.

These "micro" services are the result of several factors that include the low cost of labour compared to the price of consumer durables and capital goods, and the absence of a social security system that would take care of the non-productive population. Some of these services are to help people (personal services); others, such as maintenance and repair services, prolong the lifespan of durable consumer goods and capital goods. Micro services are a response to poverty and the necessity to split up products for clients with limited purchasing power.

- In contrast, *services to help enterprises* are knowledge and human resource intensive. Education and training, information and communication services, juridical, auditing, insurance and financial services play an essential role in the industrial sector. Overall, Africa's participation in the internationalisation of services and in technology transfer to enterprises is very weak. ❐

Creating a tertiary economy

The *tertiary sector (services)* has retained the spirit of the colonial trade for a long time and is still protected. It is the main beneficiary of economic policy measures and, since it often exists as a monopolist, it absorbs the increase in productivity of the productive sectors. Since independence, its share of the GDP has been around 40 per cent; which is a far higher percentage than the average for developing countries, while tertiary employment rose from 13 to 22,5 per cent of the economically active population between 1960 and 1990. The non-tradeables sector (prices that are not dependent on the world market) accounts for more than 50 per cent of the GDP in oil-producing countries (non-merchandised services, construction, merchandised services).

Economic dislocation

Due to a lack of infrastructure and transport networks, African economies remain *disjointed*: they consist of subsystems that do not communicate fully at the level of economic flows, prices and information. The role of the tertiary sector, often defined as that of a parasite, therefore seems contradictory. On the one hand, one can easily denounce the levy imposed by a non-productive sector that often exercises a monopoly; on the other, the absence of intermediaries usually prevents this sector from taking on the basic functions of stockpiling, the transfer of merchandise, and the meeting of supply and demand.

One can acquire a coherent understanding of the real and financial elements of Africa's macroeconomic crisis in a framework of *economic models*, that have various theoretical foundations:

- These elements can be represented through *disequilibrium models*. If one takes into account "false prices" or the failures in the transmission of market information, and supply-side constraints, one sees that African economies are constrained by the *rationing* of credit in the monetary market, of foreign currency in countries with non-convertible currencies, and of inputs on the goods market. In the labour market, the supply of non-qualified labour is infinitely elastic in relation to institutional wages. This results in distortions (in this way rationing can lead to perverted elasticities) and in transfers to parallel markets. The behaviour of private agents is linked to such *rationing*. Exchange rate control and/or a shortage of foreign currency prevents the acquisition of foreign assets. The weakness (or absence) of financial markets places a limit on financial assets. Consequently, the bulk of the possessions of the countries consists of physical assets (consumables, housing, etc.), and human assets. In the face of serious risks, private agents tend to place their savings outside the country through parallel avenues (Azam 1991; Bevan et al. 1987).
- *Post-Keynesian analyses* suggest the non-fulfilment of markets, the uncertainty of anticipation, and imperfect competition. The underdeveloped economy is one where production capacity is under-utilised, and where indelible prices are not in balance. These instabilities lead to an uncertain economic environment. Stiglitz (2002) points out the asymmetry of information, the incompleteness of markets, unstable politics and the absence of stabilising mechanisms.
- *Neo-institutionalism* aims to endogenise institutions; it introduces informational asymmetries, with coordination outside the market, reducing transaction costs and with rationing resulting from the effects of adverse selection or from incentives. It suggests the plurality of co-ordinisation modes and the role of property rights. The weakness of incentive can be explained by inadequate insititutions.
- *Neo-structuralist models* are situated in a more long-term framework; they favour a lack of interdependence, compartmen-

talisation between branches and regions, the segmentation of channels, asymmetrical relations and the absence of an environment that boosts the economy. Sectoral pluralism leads to heterogeneous prices and economic functions of agents.

The *market*, as a voluntary mechanism for transferring property rights or possessions, occupies limited space (Bohannan & Dalton 1962; Herskovits & Horowitz 1964). There are no genuine market factors; property is hardly inalienable; the majority of agents are excluded from bank credit; and financial markets are embryonic. Currencies certainly constitute valuable reserves and are accepted as payment for many goods, but they have not acquired the role of general equity enabling merchandise fundability.

Traditional African markets, which are localised and circumscribed, are radically different from global markets where capital increases. In neither of these two cases, nevertheless, is the market the self-regulating system implied by neo-classical theory.

In the *rural milieu* most agents are involved in activities that are embedded in domestic structures and are hardly integrated into the formal market economy. Producers usually sell only part of their surplus and generally favour multiple activities and food security. Most *national productive units* are in the public domain, hardly competitive, and fulfil a social function, which prevails over the logic of profitability and capital accumulation; they are coordinated through controlled prices. The role of the market is limited to the bulk of the *petty informal activities* and to the *private tertiary sector*. Traders generally exercise a monopoly and practise market sharing strategies. Finally, *the state* levies and distributes rents.

- *Calculated general equilibrium models (CGEMs)* have come to the fore. They are based on the postulation that markets function in equilibrium and that agents optimise their supply and demand decisions on the basis of real variables. As restrictions are introduced, the models become more and more "structuralist" by nature. The proliferation of these models is linked to the progress made in social compatibility matrixes, to the easier acquisition of information, and to the answers these models give to economic policy questions (trade, fiscal, social effects of structural adjustment, taking account of informal economic activities, etc.). They take into account relative prices and the role of tradeables in the international environment.

Chapter 3
External marginalisation

At the international level, internal financial imbalances arise from the deficit in the current account of the balance of payments. The end result of the rent-orientated economy and low productivity is the continued loss of external competitiveness. Besides price fluctuations, with a dynamic situation that is largely induced from the outside, Africa tends to be marginalized with regard to the main centres of the international economy.

Whatever the criteria, at the time of political *independence*, Africa was in a situation of serious economic *dependence*, indicators of which were a high level of economic openness, weak diversification of exports, and the polarisation of trade around the former metropoles (Esseks 1975). The bulk of the energy-generating products, the intermediary and capital goods, the qualified labour and training came from external sources. Foreign enterprises and administrations played a major role in the key sectors of banking, trading, transport and industry.

Since independence, external trade has lead to diversification of trading partners and a rise in the share of imported capital goods. On the other hand, exports were hardly diversified and the level of economic openness increased.

Inflationary shocks, in the aftermath of the first oil boom, facilitated access to external capital. The international credit economy found expression in the massive expansion of international loan funds. The fall in the relative share of public aid and direct investment was accompanied by a rapid growth of export credits and bank loans backed by governments. Large differences between countries were noticeable.

In contrast to the preceding decade, the *1980s* were characterised by the tightening of credit, a rise in interest rates, and a fall in the terms of trade. There was a shift in public aid, but bank loans and *direct investments* did not materialise, or were withdrawn from African countries. Northern countries no longer guaranteed loans. African countries fell into a situation of *permanent indebtedness*.

The *1990s* saw – with the exception of oil – an improvement in world commodity prices before the reversal at the end of the decade. Debt stabilised. Changes brought about by structural adjustments resulted in competitiveness gains (Sall 2000). Aid fell dramatically. Sub-Saharan Africa's exports grew in value by 7,3 per cent against a global growth of 59,9 per cent, except for South Africa, Ghana, Madagascar and Mauritius where the trend was towards concentrated exports.

3.1 International instability

The instability in terms of trade and the real value of exports had a negative effect on the growth of the global productivity factor (Géronimi, 1992). According to Guillaumont and Combe (2000), this, in addition to intermediary variables (instability of relative prices, agricultural prices and investment rates), contributed to a negative GDP growth of 0,23 per cent in Africa.

Africa has benefited from the former EEC's (today the EU's) Sugar Protocol, which guaranteed markets and prices; the Stabex Agreements for agricultural products; and the System Agreements for mineral products, which partly compensated African countries for fluctuations in export income. But there has been *an erosion of these preferential agreements*, and specialisation in products for which the global demand has grown very slowly. Preferential agreements, stabilising mechanisms, and the principles of co-operation in the Lomé Convention (1975) contradicted the rules of the World Trade Organisation (WTO). Except for specific products such as vanilla and cocoa, African countries are price *takers*, that is, their products are subject to international prices. This being the case, exchange rates have affected the profitability of different sectors and cost price competitiveness (these countries modified the export prices in their national currencies) more than they affected their retail price competitiveness (global prices are fixed) (Mainguy 1988).

The bulk of a state's income and payments for primary products and capital goods are linked to external trade (Guillaumont P. & S. 1988; Ntamatungiro 1988; Hugon et al. 1994). The economic cycles of African countries are therefore shaped by international fluctuations in exchange rates, prices, interest rates and trade flows. In fact, there has been an asymmetry of *positive and negative shocks* and low resilience to these shocks (a lack of capacity to manage and absorb shocks).

FIGURE 2: THE EFFECT OF TERMS OF TRADE CHANGES ON INCOME

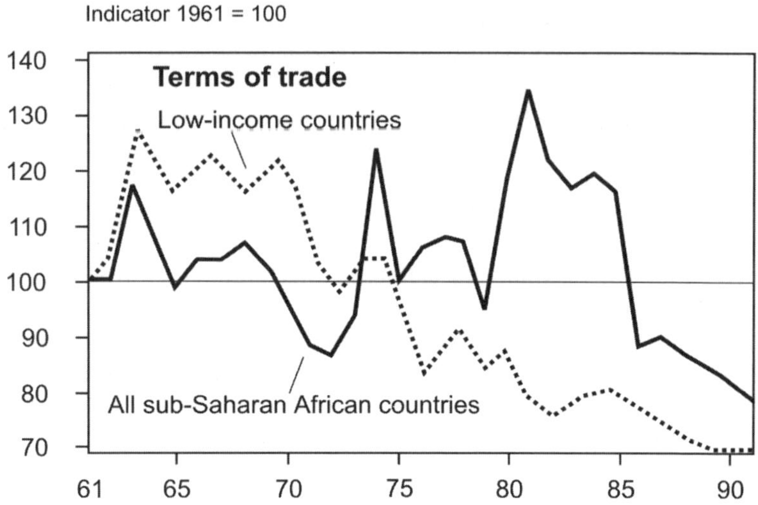

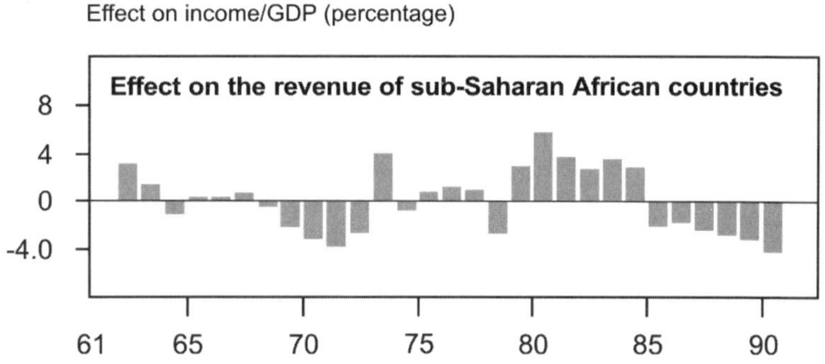

Note: These graphs illustrate the ratio of the unit value of exports and imports. They are based on a series of non-factor goods and services in current and 1980 dollars. The impact of the terms of trade variations on income for a given year is obtained by multiplying the value of non-factors goods and services exports in 1980 dollars for the year under consideration by the percentage of the terms of trade indicator variation. The result is indicated by means of a percentage of GDP in 1980 dollars for the relevant year.

Source: World Bank 1990.

During the 1970s, external instabilities as well as their transmission to the African interior increased. At the time of the *grain and oil crises* (1973–1974), most countries compensated for price explosions by subsidising consumption. Favourable export prices as well as lending capacity financed intervention strategies; these enabled the state to increase wages and created recurrent costs (the pawl effect). At first, the ebb in prices was compensated for by internal and external state-supported loans before financial insolvency led to deflationary policies. In the international arena at that time there were difficulties with the functioning of the Stabex mechanism, the disappearance of product agreements and a modification of price-fixing rules.

In the face of export income instability and consumer expenditure restrictions, adjustments took place by varying imports and investments. Eventually these fluctuations did have a retrospective effect on production and export capacity.

These external shocks had widespread repercussions, seeing that *stop-and-go macroeconomic policies* were reversible and internal stabilising measures could be lifted. Thus, in line with liberalisation, controlled prices were replaced by market prices; price stabilisation agencies, which had become institutions that raised levies, saw their role being reduced or they disappeared altogether; tariff and non-tariff protection measures were replaced by exchange rate adjustments. "Normal" instabilities, which were anticipated by agents and for which they could prepare, gave way to external shocks that created negative perceptions (Sudrie in Hugon, Pourcet & Quiers-Valette 1994). The resulting rise in uncertainty led to a slowing down in productive investment. Decision makers, confronted with an unstable environment, preferred less risky investments, thus delaying rapid capital returns to long-term productive investments. African countries also suffered from *asynchronous shocks*: thrust into an external unsynchronised economic situation they developed divergent economic policies, particularly exchange rate policies, which harmed regional trade (Coussy & Hugon 1991; Hugon 2001).

3.2 Trade marginalisation

More than 40 years after independence, African economies remain focussed on European economies, which account for more than two-thirds of the areas they trade with and from which most of their capital originates. Unlike the majority of developing countries, Africa has hardly modified the structure of its *exports*: the main primary products exported in 2000 still account for about half of all exports, as was the case in 1960; manufactured exports constitute only five per cent of total exports. In contrast, *imports* have diversified owing to the link between capital and intermediary goods with import substitution.

The linkages between Europe and Africa have led to a hub-and-spoke trading model. High-intensity transaction activities take place in the centre, whereas internal and external transaction costs in the peripheral African countries are very high. In addition, Europe (mainly the EU countries), which could stimulate growth because of size and degree of openness, has gradually moved further away from Africa.

Africa has lost *external competitiveness*:[1] its share of global trade dropped by more than half between 1970 and 2000. During the 1980s, the fall in the fixed value of exports was accompanied by a 50 per cent fall in per capita imports. Sub-Saharan Africa's exports, which made up 3,1 per cent of global exports in 1970, accounted for only 1,7 per cent in 1986 and one per cent in 2000 (of which more than 40 per cent was crude oil). Africa is facing growing competition from other developing countries, especially Asian countries. A case in point is Indonesian manufactured exports, which were lower than those of Nigeria in 1970, but were 30 times higher in 1990. With a regressive specialisation in primary products, coupled with depressed prices and bad prospects, Africa lost its share of the market for its main export crops: peanuts and peanut oil, palm oil, bananas, and rubber. It maintained its market share only for coffee, tobacco, coffee, tea, and sisal. Over a long period, its "revealed comparative advantages" became more pronounced. Those exports in the primary sector (agribusiness) rose between 1967 and 1989, in contrast to those in other manufacturing sectors (CEPII 1992).

Numerous *factors* explain this low external competitiveness in the context of the depreciation of prices (from a base of 100 in 1985, the gross terms of trade were less than 75 in 1999). In particular, the lack of external trade logistics, high transaction costs (particularly in transport and other fees), the absence of a tradition of international marketing, and structural problems in key economic sectors were at the root of Africa's weak competitiveness in an environment of imperfect competition.

Import substitution industrialisation has created an anti-export bias by raising the profitability of *non-tradeable* sectors (protected)

1 The given comparative advantages, found and transferred, should be differenciated according to the level of competition (price, volume and quality). The one type measures itself between countries for one given product, while the other type measures itself for one given country, between various products. The level of competition is subject to the macroeconomic conjuncture (especially the exchange rate); the comparative advantage is, above all, of a structural nature.

and by raising the cost of export sectors. Thus one saw a higher rate of real protection favouring imports of intermediary and capital goods, and an overvaluation of the exchange rate. With a base of 100 (1970), the real exchange rate indicator (nominal exchange rate weighed by relative prices) became 125 (mid-1980s). Factor costs in Africa were high compared to those of its competitors in other developing countries, particularly those in Asia (Sall 2000). Despite currency devaluations, labour costs remained high compared to productivity, and it often became crippling in the franc zone countries: The price of energy (with the exception of Nigeria) and trade fees in the broad sense (trade, transport, stockpiling, etc.) were often considerable. The cost of credit in the countries of the franc zone was five points higher than French rates. One also had to add to the visible costs those linked to the bureaucratic environment or to the absence of an industrial and technical infrastructure.

It is also necessary to differentiate appreciation according to *product*. Africa is relatively competitive in cotton and cocoa production, particularly on account of extensive cultivation (in the case of the Ivory Coast), though the daily wage of a planter in the Ivory Coast is higher than that of a planter in Malaysia. The weak competitiveness of rice in Africa is largely the result of downstream costs (trade, transport, processing). In the case of palm oil, industrial plantation production costs are twice as high in the Ivory Coast as in Malaysia (1990 figures).

With a few rare exceptions, *trade liberalisation*, which has taken place since the 1980s, has not resulted in a recovery of exports. A reduction and change in the structure of imports (to the benefit of consumer goods and the detriment of capital goods) can be observed during the period of import liberalisation and of lower real exchange rates. The elasticity of exports and imports in relation to the GDP (1,45 and 1,33 respectively between 1965 and 1980) has tended to decrease markedly in the context of adjustment and liberalisation. It fell to 0,09 and –2,4 between 1980 and 1989 (CERED).

The least developed countries (LDCs) have liberalised their trade more than other developing countries. In 1999, 37 per cent of the 43 LDCs had duties below 20 per cent with zero or insignificant non-tariff barriers as opposed to 23 per cent for the 78 other developing countries.

African countries are up against trade obstacles with regard to industrialised countries. Losses are estimated at US$2,5bn for developing countries. The European Union's "Everything But Arms" deal and the United States' Africa Growth and Opportunity Act may have some positive effects. It is nevertheless necessary to take into account supply capacity, the risk of trade diversion, Africa being a "Trojan Horse" for third world countries or multinational corporations (MNCs), which necessitates certification and complex "rules of origin".

If one takes into the account the share of imported inputs in the exports of processed products, or the share of "call products" (imported consumer goods) in providing incentives for agricultural export production, foreign currency shortages have generally acted as a disincentive to exports (Berthelemy & Morrisson 1991).

Some tests have shown that the weak integration of the global market (over-evaluation of the real exchange rate, non-tariff barriers, low share of manufactured products in exports, low assessment of solvency, and low rate of foreign direct investment) would have had a negative impact on growth. An over-valuation, estimated at 86 per cent between 1976 and 1985, would have reduced the annual growth rate by between 1,5 and 2,1 per cent. The subsequent depreciation of the exchange rate did not seem to stimulate growth either.

3.3 Permanent indebtedness

During the 1980s, sub-Saharan Africa was caught in a spiral of *permanent indebtedness* (Raffinot & Moisseron 2000). Credit had to be guaranteed on the basis of real asset growth, but, in fact, capital flight and the financing of "cathedrals in the desert" or of projects that created an excess capacity to produce primary products had generally not enabled the creation of profitable real assets. Africa thus became a place where capital was recycled, which, in turn, gave way to money laundering and the financing of foreign political parties or over-invoicing, a source of private and public rents.

In the context of low added value to primary goods and high interest rates, most borrowing countries became *insolvent* debtors. Debt rescheduling and access to credit to pay back interest have led to an accumulation of arrears and have transferred the bulk of the debt, with the latter becoming an independent item in relation to the real economy. *External debt* (US$210bn, excluding South Africa) tripled between 1980 and 1988; it rose from 97 per cent to 177 per cent of exports of goods and services, and from 27 per cent to 61 per cent of the GDP. Debt servicing, after rescheduling, rose (in percentage of goods and services exports) from 11 per cent to 15,1 per cent, of which about half was in the form of interest repayments. The countries most affected by this increase were middle-income countries subject to lower prices for primary goods (Ivory Coast, Cameroon, Congo, Gabon), as well as Highly-Indebted Poor Countries (Senegal, Madagascar, former Zaire). African countries have been caught in a debt spiral or debt trap, and the issue is one of high indebtedness and its non-sustainability. Debt, mainly public, has a retrospective effect on internal public debt – it is a sword of Damocles. The Highly-Indebted Poor Countries (HIPC) initiative, launched in 1996 and extended in Cologne in 1999, has broadened the spectrum of debt to include multilateral debt. It is furthering the reversal of indebtedness without conditionalities by encouraging countries to embark on a poverty-reduction strategy. In 2003, 22 countries made use of the initiative. The drop in indebtedness represents 2,7 per cent of GDP (1,2 per cent if one takes into account the reductions). The cost of cancelling the debts of the developing countries is estimated at US$36,7bn (nominal value) and at US$20,3bn (net present value, that is, in terms of the value of future reimbursements). The debt of the developing countries represents 100 per cent of their GNP.

The net flows of long-term capital into LDCs have diminished by 25 per cent overall in nominal terms, and by 39 per cent in real value since 1990, dropping from US$14,2bn in 1991 to US$10,4 in 1998. This decline has been due to a decline in aid. The share of aid in the GDP of developing countries has dropped from 0,09 per cent in 1990 to 0,05 per cent in 1998. Private capital has increased due to foreign direct investment in oil-producing countries (Angola, Equatorial Guinea).

External debt levels increased during the nineties. In developing countries these rose from US$121bn in 1990 to US$150bn in 1998. Most African countries remain highly indebted. Sub-Saharan Africa (with the exception of South Africa) is hardly affected by private international capital flows, or the risks linked to their volatility. Of 420 large subsidiaries in Africa in 1999, 60 per cent were European (of which 45 per cent were French subsidiaries mainly in the countries in its sphere of influence).

With the exception of a few sectors, such as oil or agribusiness, *private foreign investors* have adopted a wait-and-see policy: the market has stagnated and *multinational companies* have withdrawn. Between 1980 and 1996 foreign direct investment into Africa represented two per cent of total global investment, as opposed to 30 per cent for Asia, despite the implementation of measures to attract investment such as investment codes and privatisation. This can be explained by several factors such as political instability, narrow markets, and serious risks. The rates of return on investments of subsidiaries of large American companies were estimated at close to 30 per cent compared to less than 20 per cent for other developing countries. Companies exporting primarily mineral, energy, or agricultural products dominated the market. Few companies *subcontracted* for export purposes despite the appearance of free trade zones (Mauritius, Senegal, Madagascar and Togo). Except for large markets such as Nigeria or South Africa, import substitution companies suffered from the effects of market contraction (departure of expatriates, fall in income of the middle classes) and from competition from smuggling.

In the year 2000, the net per capita capital inflow was half what it had been at the beginning of the 1980s. Private flows represented only 20 per cent of the region's GNP. Forty per cent of net capital inflows went back to creditor countries in the form of interest payments or the repatriation of profits.

Fall in public aid

As a result of the drying up of private flows, *overseas development assistance* (ODA) increased (Adda & Smouts 1990; Gabas 1990, Magnard & Tenzer 1988). This partly eased external financial constraints. Surveys conducted for the period 1980 to 1987 in 30 African countries show that investment rates were positively linked to the overall rise in aid. Aid, however, has a weak absorption capacity: it is often diverted from its purpose and has limited multiplier effects (for every 100 inflows, 60 immediately leave again). It also has negative effects: there is bias in favour of capital-intensive projects and recurrent costs. In 2002, aid represented 6,2 per cent of Africa's GDP. Since the fall of the Berlin Wall aid to Africa has tended to drop: it fell from US$14bn in 1990 to less than US$10bn in 2000.

Owing both to the balance of payments and public finance deficits, external aid (subsidies, loans) has become more macroeconomic and less project based. Because of the bias towards *counterpart funds*, it is used to relax foreign currency shortages in particular and/or to ensure the financing of minimal budgetary expenditures. Where aid is used in this way, it allows these countries just to keep their heads above water, but takes responsibility away from the authorities and seems to be linked to debt: it is as if the authorities have been put under supervision.

ODA dropped by 30 per cent in nominal terms and by 45 per cent per capita during the 1990s. ODA of US$16,7bn to the LDCs in 1990 stood at US$11,6bn ten years later. *Aid fatigue* has become noticeable.

Aid has often been inefficient because of the proliferation of donors, the weak integration of projects, and high volatility (higher than the income of some states from trade according to the UNCTAD 2000 report).

Debt and aid go hand in hand and have created a vicious circle. Debt has reduced the efficiency of aid and, in turn, more aid has been given to indebted countries and has increased the debt burden.

Aid has created a bias in favour of capital expenditures at the expense of functional expenditures. Nevertheless, it plays an important role. In Mali it has made up 80 per cent of public expenditure, 20 per cent of the GNP and 50 per cent of imports during the past two decades.

The dismantling of aid decided upon at the LDC conference in Brussels in May 2001, may have positive effects by reducing import costs – on condition that it does not become a disincentive to donors.

With the exception of Nigeria and South Africa, African economies that do not have internal markets allowing for economies of scale, are *impoverished* by their *specialisation* in exporting low value-added goods in the face of a stagnating world demand. Considered strategically unimportant, African countries face two sources of competition: firstly from Eastern European countries at the level of the priority of financial flows, and also from Asian and Latin American countries that produce similar export products. This marginalisation is evidence of the gradual erosion of an economy based on colonial trade, poor specialisation, the receipt of aid from and being thrust into a global economy that is undergoing serious changes (such as interconnecting markets and the information revolution).

Historically, African countries have thus reaped little benefit from Europe's dissemination of its growth model through technology transfers, direct investments, and the opening of European markets for industrial products, and this has led to price escalation. They have rarely been able to create new comparative advantages and control their access to the external world through a combination of rigorous macroeconomic and selective industrial policies. The counter-example is that of the integrated cotton sector in francophone Africa, which has risen from four per cent of the global market (1980) to nine per cent (1990) and on to 16 per cent (1997).

In its long history, Africa has always been an open market, owing to efficient trade networks historically revolving around gold, slaves, primary products and somewhat illicit activities. Today it is partially integrated into a similar global economy (arms sales, drug trafficking, money laundering – all of which are simultaneously sources of private enrichment and violent conflicts) (Bayart et al. 1989; Vallée & Missen 1999; Mbembé 2000). This has hardly created comparative advantages in innovative sectors. One would expect new communication and information technologies to offer opportunities, but technological leaps are difficult. The acquisition of new technologies is hampered by poor telecommunication networks, the high cost of these technologies, and the impoverished human resources needed to master these technologies.

PART TWO
ECONOMIC RATIONALITIES AND SOCIO POLITICAL CONTEXT

It is not trade that comes first, but community ties (Merina proverb).

The pot starts boiling from the bottom (Ibo proverb).

The preceding macroeconomic framework is doubly reductionist. It does not take into account either social permanence (e.g. trans-frontier trade networks), or the changing practices of agents. The African landscape, which is very variable, has changed considerably since independence. Africa has become more densely populated and urbanised: it has formed an elite and has seen, since 1980, an improvement in most social indicators. The way in which space is occupied has been transformed and cities are characterised by dynamic informal trading activities. The true levels of the satisfaction of basic needs cannot be compared to what is disclosed by per capita income indicators. It is important to take into account in particular the *unreliability of information systems, the scale of the phenomena under investigation* and their *temporality*, and to analyse economic rationality in a specific socio-political context.

When one regards Africa from a *microeconomic* vantage point, and with a different conception of time, the landscape becomes more varied; "internal dynamics" (Balandier 1971) come to the fore above macroeconomic flows and accounting balances. Since independence, Africans have been able to manage, in their own way, a doubling of their population, a fivefold increase in their urban population, the putting into place of state institutions and the maintenance of borders constituting nation-states despite their artificial nature and cross-border ethnic divisions. This need for a micro approach is also the result of the new division of roles between state and market in regulating the economy. Indicative planning and steering by the state has disappeared. Hence, it is necessary to arrive at a more subtle understanding of household behaviour, decentralised decision-making levels and the practices of different role-players.

The "role players at the bottom" of the economy (Bayart 1989) have invented, innovated, and created activities to satisfy numerous basic needs. *The microeconomic rationality* of these people is linked to their membership in networks and social structures that give rise to atypical behaviour (Chapter 4). The means of regulating distribution conflicts lead to the *logic of redistribution* (Chapter 5). *Productive dynamics* can be found at a demographic, migratory, and scholarly level (Chapter 6). One sees this rationale being questioned in relation to a disregard for the modes of regulation, with indeed some disintegration of social networks.

In African societies where capitalism did not subordinate itself to different sectors of society, family-orientated systems have remained the society's matrix. *Homo economicus* certainly acts in his own interest; he is rational and relational. His rationality is contextual. He acts in a context where constraints are relaxed (under-employment, abundant soil, removed from the border of efficiency). These societies are more holistic than industrial societies that are dominated by individualism.

Chapter 4
Microeconomic behaviour

The *behaviour* of stakeholders generally does not lead to the outcomes expected by orthodox economics. Consumers often respond less to price incentives than to norms; producers show atypical supply behaviour (income effect where supply dwindles when prices rise, inelasticity and instability of supply in relation to prices). Consumption levels do not conform to official income.

According to Hircshmann, as soon as *family networks*, evasion practices or the *exit option*, and population instability are integrated, one has to ultimately reverse standard microeconomic hypotheses. Individual and collective decision-making units have consumption and expenditure constraints linked to obligations (housing dependants, transfers, etc.). Choices consequently revolve around income (multiple activities, rural or urban incomes, informal or formal wages).

4.1 Is *Homo africanus* rational?

The anthropological tradition

The *anthropological tradition* postulates the primacy of the social act, which cannot be reduced to individual phenomena, and the nonpertinence of *Homo economicus* in "primitive", threatened or underdeveloped societies. The archetype of Western rationality is specific to merchant societies alone. The behaviour of stakeholders, therefore, is understood by taking into account social structures and value systems.

Thus, *tontines* can be interpreted as a total benefits system, about which Mauss states: "Here one trades in money and labour; but also in meals; in rites, particularly mourning; in friendship obligations; and in advice. The contract that binds members is indeed more than a jurisdiction; it is also religious and mythological" (Henry et al. 1990).

Many African authors emphasise the incompatibility between African *perception* and Western reason (individualism, organisation, productivity, accumulation) (Elunga 1990; Latouche 1998; Engelhardt 1998). In traditional *rural societies*, there is no distinction between the sacred and the profane; all economic and social activities are subject to ritual. Nature expresses itself through the forces that reflect it. Consequently, there is a close link between man and nature, both of whom partake of the same vital force. The ancestors live in symbiosis with the living; time is not continuous: sacred time is linked to profane time, it is divided into activities differentiated by type; cyclical time recurs according to the rhythm of the seasons. Linked to a disregard for the future is the value attributed to the world beyond. Ultimately, one would prefer investing in a grave, for one dies forever; rather than in material goods, since life is ephemeral. Destiny is seen as an actualisation of the forefathers' project.

Consequently, the economic and material act that has lost its sacred aura takes a secondary place. The profane use of an article is less important than its sacred use. The ambivalent time dedicated to traditional activities prevails over productive time. The gift and the counter-gift are "exchanges that differ in difference" which are in contrast by virtue of their time limit and their sense of equivalent relations in market trade (cf. the Biloba at the Fang). According to Lévi-Strauss, the society is a system of symbolic relations before it is a system of onerous exchanges.

Economic "irrationality" could therefore explain the absence of any priority given to the economic act in relation to social or symbolic activities, the valuation of human beings and interpersonal relations. According to Hyden (1980), African behaviour can be explained by the logic of the *emotional economy* where reciprocal understanding is based on ties of parentage, origin or religion. Many studies explain the very low productivity of African societies through the disappearance of surplus caused by social channels (Berry 1985). Surplus produced in a merchandised environment disappears in the traditional environment. Traits that are considered virtues according to community logic (polygamy, solidarity and respect of norms) become vices under the efficiency logic (nepotism, clientilism and tribalism).

The substantial rationality of *Homo economicus*

Conversely, the objective of *orthodox economists* is to analyse economic behaviour independent of social structure, by postulating the universality of motive (utilitarianism), of operating modes (substantial rationality), and of market coordination. *Formalist anthropologists* also adhere to the postulation of *substantial rationality*. Thus, the most popular technique appears to be rational as long as labour is scarce; the collective consumption of cattle, linked to ceremonial sacrifices, is the best way to use perishable goods; similarly, high fertility can be linked to the rationality of producing a labour force or of security in old-age, and so on.

According to orthodox economics, economic stakeholders respond to price changes and are individual economic units. That being the case, the toolbox of "standard" instruments can be used, from *rational forecasting* through to price-income elasticities and the logic of *optimisation*. According to Koulibaly (1992), it is important to start off with the preferences and buying power of stakeholders. African underdevelopment is the main result of community pressures and the drain on incomes and distortions caused by the state. The community, an anthropological fiction, has to be analysed subjectively according to the choices of individuals who belong to several communities and, therefore, from the perspective of *methodological individualism*.

Other economists suggest *rationing* as the a priori explanation of atypical behaviour; in a rural environment, supply cannot be separated from the demand function of workers if the latter are subject to rationing of consumer goods. Consequently, price rises do not necessarily stimulate supply (Berthelemy & Morrison 1991). Threshold effects can be observed (below a certain level, price instability reduces production, whereas above that level it enhances production).

4.2 Rules, norms and uncertain decisions

It is important to move beyond this debate between the irrationality of *Homo africanus* and the rationality of *Homo economicus*. One can use the theory of *individual choice in a situation of imperfect and asymmetrical information* (risk and uncertainty) or the theory of *property rights* and explicit or implicit *contracts*, and the role of *rules* and *conventions* in the context of radical uncertainty (Hugon, Pourcet & Quiers-Valette 1994). African stakeholders (peasants and informal producers) follow the approach of *risk* minimisation, depending on their social positions. Parents who invest in schooling, producers who cultivate multiple crops, or urban migrants estimate an anticipated personal income and reason in terms of a calculated gain or utility. Stakeholders (or nations) have an interest in extensive rather than intensive cultivation, and in the diversification of their portfolios instead of specialisation.

In an *uncertain* environment, stakeholders simultaneously favour the *short-term* market and *intergenerational* investments. They make short-term choices that leave the greatest number of future options open. Consequently, there is a strong preference for liquidity, and the maintenance of a range of available options in comparison with the irreversibility of the physical investment decision and the maintenance of monetary and financial assets at the expense of productive assets. The daily struggle leads to a very strong preference for *current interest rates* – the reason why they are also excessively high. Societies that are not very productive are characterised by instability, low life expectancy, insecurity and precariousness, which prevents a long-term view and leads to a preference for the immediate. This approach is, however, equally valid for the long-term view of community membership. In the absence of the *welfare state*, the idea of community reduces uncertainty. The rules of the tontine allow for immediate cash withdrawal in the face of a risky event. These benefit/redistribution mechanisms are an insurance system. Families thus enhance the value of the distant future and therefore have a long-term vision, sacrificing themselves for their children; parents prefer to invest in the welfare of their children. The domestic or "household" unit is a centre of collective decision making with, one can assume, an infinite intergenerational vision and whose discount rate is nil even if that of each of its components is positive.

The ideal of *Homo africanus* is thus as inadequate as that of *Homo economicus*. As Mahieu (1990) points out, the satisfaction of collective obligations or the community imperative is a prerequisite for the utilitarian calculation, which thus becomes residual; every person has an interest in redistribution, so that the greatest advantage for the most destitute represents only a small sacrifice for the most privileged (Rawls' Rule of Maximin). The utilitarian calculation at the heart of the *membership* of communities combines with the imposed norms of *belonging* for every community. Identity that justifies social ties has become much more meaningful since the crisis modified social policies and since the decline of the state. These variable identities are themselves subject to evolution and negotiation, even if history has materialised these perceived identities as essential differences (Ivory nationality, Hutu or Tutsi ethnicity).

4.3 Atypical economic behaviour

This approach leads to specific econometric relations, which can be illustrated by the examples below.

- *Consumer budget reports* lead to some results that conform to the orthodox theory of price or income elasticity. Food is inferior, with an income elasticity below one, whereas non-foodstuffs have an income elasticity of more than one. On the other hand, related consumer structures (very briefly summarised) and income levels between countries with a per capita income below US$1 500 does not illustrate Engel's law. Depending on the country, transport, housing, education and health are the most important needs. *Poverty effects* are characterised by the substitution of products consumed by the poor (starches and roots) for products consumed by those who are richer (meat, dairy products, cereals). Demonstration effects can also be observed.

- In cities, "traditional" society imposes consumption norms that cannot be transgressed, even if "modern" society favours new practices.
- The *ethnic determinant* is important. *Savings rates* vary largely according to ethnic group in the Ivory Coast (from nil to 15 per cent for the Arditi and Yung respectively).
- *Labour supply* depends on several factors. The effect of income comes into play below certain thresholds. It is believed that if people are paid more they work less. Earning a wage is sometimes a temporary activity allowing one to meet monetary obligations (e.g. payment of the dowry). A reinterpretation of former referents leads to plural interlocking logics. The plurality of rights expresses this diversity of referents (Lebris et al. 1982). The economy, functioning through networks, is evidence of mutual co-operation relations, reciprocity, gifts and counter-gifts, and geographical proximity (Baron 1994; Latouche 1998), but it also attests to antagonism.
- The supply of cotton in the franc zone is not as much linked to the price level as it is to the stability of real prices and to related transactions.

At the collective level such atypical individual behaviour can lead to *compounding effects* (differences between individual intentions and collective outcomes):

- thus, the anticipation of high private earnings, which explains the demand for schooling, leads to an inflated number of graduates and to over-schooling, when one takes account of the ability of students to find employment and to finance themselves. The demand of families for children as an old-age insurance nevertheless ends up in a demographic explosion that has negative effects;
- the individual rationale of extensive cultivation (minimisation of risks, labour-force savings, land ownership strategies in anticipation of soil scarcity, etc.) increases the degradation

Economic rationality and African organisations

The debate between the *holistic* view of the anthropological tradition and the *individualistic* view of the microeconomic tradition can obviously not be resolved scientifically. There are three main factors that greatly influence the assumptions of accepted rationality.

- Economic rationality cannot be separated from the *market and capitalist context*. It is linked to the concept of competition. Thus, according to Hayek (1980), there is a "supposition, not that most or even all market participants are rational, but to the contrary that a small number of relatively more rational individuals will, through competition, force the others to emulate them". This is not the case with African societies. Economic stakeholders are generally not constrained either by competition and accumulation or by innovation and "creative destructiveness". Paradoxically, in this sense liberalisation can reinforce security-seeking behaviour instead of promoting the emergence of entrepreneurs.
- The black box of *collective decision-making units and organisations* also needs opening up. In informal units, the budgets of production units cannot be dissociated from those of domestic units.

of *ecosystems*. Peasants and cattle owners inhabiting the Sahel "destroy their environment to try to slow down their own destruction".

The response of stakeholders to the same price incentives can lead to *compounding sophisms* (excess agricultural supply causing a fall in prices).

If one takes into account the preference for liquidity and the difference in profit rates between productive investments and financial or speculative investments (property, import-export, and external investments), one sees that those owning capital favour financial and market activities at the expense of activities that would

Households are generally not the basic decision-making units in lineage and matriarchal/matrilineal systems: consumption, distribution and accumulation units are not all the same (Gastellu 1979). Those who make decisions relating to fertility are not the same as those who have to suffer its consequences. Consequently, everybody belongs to several decision-making centres: family, lineage and group membership.

- *Social networks* (based on kinship, ethnicity, or religion) affect relations between individual household members and the external world. Linear and ethnic structures, quite unlikely to transform with modernity into structures comparable to Western structures, seem to be strengthened. Diverse solidarity networks and redistribution mechanisms are essential modes of regulation and explain behaviour in times of crisis.

One should bear in mind that the degree of coherence and social integration, and attachment to the norms on which the community bases its existence, is much more important than an uncertain, threatening environment which can have catastrophic consequences. African societies have historically survived on the basis of "traditions" consisting of norms, constraints, attributive and distributive rules, and sanctions imposed on the individual. ❐

lead to a sustainable expansion of the market and to productive accumulation.

According to Simon, economic stakeholders have a "limited rationality"; they only look for acceptable or satisfying solutions. Admittedly, most modes of co-operation can in part be explained by the reduction in transaction costs. The personalisation of ethnic relations allows for close sources of confidence. Social linkages are characterised by overlapping debts in the linear hierarchy or protective networks, or by clientilism. The accumulation of *social capital* and *linkages* (investing in the social network) often prevails over the accumulation of *goods.*

Chapter 5
Redistribution logic

In "pre-industrial" societies, as in "post-industrial" societies, labour relations do not drive social relations. Only a very small part of the population has access to formal training, professional and social security protection systems. The conditions determining the use and productivity of the labour force are found outside of the wage relationship. Modes of *regulation* (all the procedures capable of ensuring social cohesion through the resolution of conflicts around income distribution) refer to rent sharing and the logic of redistribution, which can be analysed in terms of *transfers*.

5.1 Income and poverty

The way in which African *poverty* is portrayed is quite paradoxical. On the one hand, images of famine, urban misery, and children with bloated stomachs prevail; per capita income and social indicators paint an "objective" picture of the poverty afflicting the majority and the wealth of the few. In the Ivory Coast, the richest 20 per cent of the population receives 62 per cent of income. Poverty affects half the continent's population. The usual income indicators show that Africa is characterised by extreme situations. In 1990, of 29 developing countries, nine had a Gini coefficient of above 0,5 (very high inequality); the country with the most even income distribution, South Korea, has a Gini coefficient of 0,36. Thus some Gini indicators in Africa were below or equal to 0,41 (Benin, Chad, Togo), while others were above 0,6 (Kenya, Swaziland, Zambia, Zimbabwe). Those in the Ivory Coast, Tanzania, and Senegal (Bourguignon & Morrisson 1992) are in-between. The poverty elasticity to economic growth ratio is about –2.

On the other hand, an observer would note that, with some exceptions, markets are well stocked and well supplied; social networks and *redistribution mechanisms* seem to function even though some people are excluded from community networks and state handouts. It appears that the allocation of community and state *rent income* have to be taken into account (Mahieu 1990). Redistribution and corruption mean very different things to different social categories. For those at the "bottom" they are a means of survival, whereas for those at the "top" they contribute towards capital flight.

Nevertheless, despite redistribution mechanisms, the noticeable drop in income since the 1980s has led to pauperisation, and even to critical situations in countries at war. The percentage of the population of the Ivory Coast living below the poverty line rose from 11 per cent in 1985 to 31 per cent in 1993 and to 37 per cent in 1995 (Tapinos, Hugon & Vimard 2001). Average life expectancy has stagnated between 1995 and 2003 and has fallen in southern Africa.

5.2 Productive units and informal economic activity

Heterogeneity of production units

Weak intermediary technologies and Small and Medium Enterprises (*missing middle*) are characteristic of *dualist* African economies. African *enterprises* are generally managed in a relational mode; productivity does not seem to be a priority. Historically, the establishment of companies has been the result of voluntary state action or external aid, and hardly that of endogenous entrepreneurial dynamics. This has been linked to power relations and the redistribution approach of network membership.

Foreign companies follow a profit-making approach, but they are often semi-monopolies. On the one hand, they make up for the state's weakness by taking responsibility for collective goods and services (energy and infrastructure); but on the other they benefit from situational rents owing to their links with the incumbent powers or their niche positioning.

Public companies and parastatals, which initially were substitutes for private entrepreneurs, in many instances have become regulators of graduate unemployment, in fact, prebondary institutions collecting stipends (Ethiopian Airlines or many cotton companies are counter-examples).

This structure discouraged a collective ethos of promoting efficiency, entrepreneurship, and the reversibility implicit in industrial investment (Favereau in Hugon et al. 1994). Producers respond to four main approaches: a *domestic* approach to customary norms

EVOLUTION OF HUMAN DEVELOPMENT INDICATORS IN AFRICA SINCE INDEPENDENCE

PROGRESS	REGRESSION
Life expectancy	
Life expectancy was 48,9 years in 1998, that is, 8,9 years more than in 1960.	There are three life-threatening situations in areas that are enveloped in chaos (epidemics, wars, famines).
Health	
Forty-eight per cent of the population has access to health services as opposed to 30 per cent in 1960. Forty per cent of the population has access to drinkable water as opposed to 27 per cent in 1960. Public expenditure on health rose from 0,7 per cent of the GDP to 1 per cent in 1990.	Of 33 million people infected by HIV/Aids in 2000, two-thirds are in sub-Saharan Africa. Per capita expenditure on social services has fallen without an adequate inflow of private finance.
Feeding and nutrition	
The food dependency coefficient (imports/consumption) of 13,1 per cent in 1960 dropped to 10 per cent in 1990.	The calorie intake was 89 per cent of the normal level in 1997 as opposed to 92 per cent in 1965.
Education	
The literacy rate is 51 per cent, as opposed to 27 per cent in 1970. The consolidated primary and secondary education rate is 46 per cent, as opposed to 26 per cent in 1970. Public expenditure on education was 1,3 per cent of the GNP in 1960, reaching 6,1 per cent in 1998.	There is a marked deterioration in the quality of teaching and an exodus of skilled workers (more than 60 000 middle and senior managers between 1985 and 1990). The gross primary education rate, which was 80 per cent in 1980, was 75 per cent in 1995.
Women	
The gap between the sexes has been reduced with regard to the levels of education, literacy and access to basic needs.	Fifty three per cent of women are illiterate as against only 34 per cent of men.
Children	
The mortality rate of children younger than 5 years (28,4 per cent in 1960) had fallen to 17,2 per cent by 1998.	More than one million children are infected with HIV/Aids (4 million orphans).
Income	
The adjusted real per capita GDP* of US$644 in 1960 reached US$1520 in 1998.	Real wages dropped by more than a quarter between 1970 and 1998. The annual per capita GNP growth rate of 1,5 per cent (1965–1980) fell to –1,7 per cent (1980–1989) and to –0,4 per cent (1990–1998).

* Cf. the definition on page 7.
Sources: UNDP 2000, World Bank 2000.

(solidarity, reciprocity); a *market* approach to short-term market profitability (equivalence); a *controlled* approach to security through redistribution mechanisms (hierarchy); and an *industrial* approach involving calculated risk by the investor who anticipates a long-term technical trend (accumulation) (Hugon 1989).

In a rural environment, faced with the technical expertise rationality of development organisations, who are disseminating technological innovation and advocating intensification and specialisation, peasants abide by rules (ensuring or having historically ensured the continuity of the system) that allow them to manage uncertainty, avoid exclusion and have access to land. Thus they prefer extensive cultivation.

Informalisation of the economy

Frequent crises have led to the emergence of an *informal* African economy (Hugon et al. 1977; Deblé & Hugon 1981). This, owing to ambiguity and ambivalence, is loaded with contradictions. On account of the decline in employment creation in the public and parastatal sectors, and the absence of shift work in the modern private sector, the informal sector plays an increasingly important role. The latter can be defined as a set of small-scale organisations where there are no (or a limited number of) wage earners, where capital input is low, but where money nevertheless circulates and commercial goods and services are produced. Wage rules, rather than customary, hierarchical, and paternalistic rules prevail.

The majority of the population lives and survives through the *urban mass economy,* (Bugnicourt 1971; Engelhardt 1998), which is a space of innovation and ingenuity. It enables them to satisfy basic needs that are not covered by formal systems: food, housing, clothing, education, care, transport and recreation. The informal sector consists of *female* activities such as feeding-related activities (distribution, preparation and trading), personal and bodily needs; and *male* activities such as repairs, the reclamation and recycling of industrial products, transport, processing and manufacturing.

Taking account of the informal sector has called into question *dualist models* that turn the traditional, rural or subsistence sector into a supplier of low-wage labour for the modern sector. It has also led to the questioning of standard categories and an analysis of the many-sided nature of labour laws: risks, multiple activities, and family or caste dependence. There is an infinite variety of small traders in accordance with opportunity, clients, or access to supplies. Owing to their immense heterogeneity, they have to be differentiated into several strata, especially with regard to survival and small market production activities.

Rationality and accumulation in a rural environment

Some rural societies give priority to seeking equality between members by dissipating *surplus* (consumption studied by Bataille). Serer egalitarianism (Senegal) (Gastellu 1979) thus encourages simple production methods. Disparities nevertheless arise from modernisation projects (cultivation through the use of ploughing animals/agricultural mechanisation). For the big planters in the Ivory Coast, studied by Affrou Yapi, wealth is not an end in itself, but a means of attaining power. In a number of chiefdoms the obvious logic is that of accumulating prestige by increasing the number of dependants and the control over men and livestock. This logic can give rise to equalising mechanisms; thus, in the south-east of Madagascar, chiefs who have accumulated livestock have to sacrifice these until the herd is decimated and new chiefs emerge. Conversely, it can seem to be a "primitive accumulation" mechanism: the El Hadj in the north of Nigeria, like the inhabitants of the Comoros Islands who organise large weddings, use symbolic capital investment as a means of establishing a network of dependants, who are a source of trade profits and of cheap capital accumulation.

Consequently, restrictive traditions should not be opposed to the modernity of the monetary economy. Generally, African societies that are apparently most open to the "modernity" of the monetary economy, the profit logic and the market, have the most rigid social structures and are characterised by inflexible modes of consumption and the importance of community transfers. The motivation of Bamileke entrepreneurs (Cameroon) can therefore be explained by the role of common heritage, the limitations of reciprocity, and the role of customs and membership of associations. ❐

There are several *characteristics*: the young age of breadwinners; the low entry barriers into various sectors because of the ability to put up money collected through personal savings; the use of simple technologies and non-wage-related social relations. The lack of accounting skills and the poor differentiation between the production unit and the domestic unit precludes the assumption that maximising the gross outcome of one's labour is the main objective. Those who draw a surplus generally look to diversify their activities. Since money is a scarce factor, small producers want to maximise their returns in relation to their monetary expenditure. They are subjected to risky supplies and fragmented and fluctuating market outlets. Consequently they want to transfer part of the risk to the environment, internalise some transactions at the level of domestic units, and absorb shocks (use of family labour, the diversification approach) (Pourcet 1979).

On the one hand, informal (small) producers are embedded in networks characterised by confidential and cooperative interpersonal relations and are linked to *domestic* units (non-separation of domestic and production budgets, use of family labour, dilution of surplus in families) (Pourcet in Hugon et al. 1994). On the other hand, however, they are integrated into the *market* and subject to competition; small units appear and disappear very quickly.

The change from an informal unit to a small and medium enterprise presupposes a change in organisation, submitting to formal rules, attaining visibility, and internalising entrepreneurial risks. Consequently, one sees the logic of favouring diversification rather than intensive accumulation, which would enable a significant increase in production. Yet, the informal sector is the main social and economic regulator and an indicator of the potential the future holds. While it may seem hazardous to turn it into a training ground for highly efficient enterprises, it cannot merely be reduced to unproductive survival activities. Its future potential is nevertheless largely linked to that of the state, which has to take on the financing of an enabling environment, and to that of the modern sector (supply of inputs and outlets).

In some cases dynamic processes develop around industrial districts and innovative and entrepreneurial environments, and around linkages between industrial and micro-units. Often, a myriad of petty informal activity is a testimony to ingenuity; it allows a greater number of people to satisfy their basic needs. Conversely, unintentional innovations may appear in places that are becoming marginalised or as a response to urban pauperisation; these survival strategies translate into a fallback on identity.

5.3 Community and state transfers

Community transfers

The wider *family* remains the core of African society. It is the principal location of goods and subsistence production, of continuing production, and of labour supply for the market. *Intergenerational and inter-group transfers* tend to compensate for the absence of unemployment insurance and social protection.

These networks carry four main advantages: the reduction of transaction costs; the optimisation of risk management through organisation into groups; the reduction of apprenticeship costs; and, sometimes, the substitution of training by the private sector. Nevertheless, the personalisation of relations and the effects of proximity prevent economies of scale and often hamper fast adaptation to change.

According to Mahieu (1990), there is a set of *rights* (implicit through non-exclusion and explicit regarding goods, people and time) and *obligations*. The allocation of time cannot simply be summarised as a comparison between the income and marginal productivity of each agent. Arbitration between the domestic and market spheres, between wage earners and informal workers, or between near and distant activities results from taking into account the rights and obligations linked to each social status.

Transfers, at the heart of communities and intergenerational groups, play an important role in the satisfaction of basic needs. An estimated 60 per cent of households in Abidjan make direct and indirect transfers (pastoral care, accommodation, etc.). Similarly, the Soninke society (in Senegal) or the Mossi (in Burkina Faso) basically live from emigrant incomes. This approach is essential in understanding food security (largely linked to migrant rights), human investment (especially education expenditures), and savings mechanisms (the tontine is a way of protecting one's savings when faced with community pressures).

Multidimensional *poverty*, which cannot be reduced to income (World Bank 2000), can be attributed to a reduction of rights linked to *exclusion* from markets, public goods, and networks of community membership (Sen 1981). The question arises whether, in a context of urban crises and catastrophes (war, HIV/Aids), there is a tendency towards individualism as a source of exclusion.

State rent

Community transfers can be explained at the macroeconomic level by the creation, circulation and allocation of surplus or *state rent*.

The latter is basically the result of external relations: financial transfers, levies on trade of exported products, royalties or import duties (Bayart 1989). An analysis of redistribution allows one to reconsider the ambivalent role of the *state* (Médard 1991), which is subject to rent withdrawal deprivation strategies, capital flight, and taking back positions occupied by foreigners; it is at the same time dependent on and in conflict with the external world. In the absence of social security systems or the access of stakeholders to a number of goods through the market, it plays a redistributing role, relying on clientele networks and community membership. The African state feeds on its external relations to sustain compromises or finance internal conflicts. In the face of the failures of the African state, "civil society", that is all those forces that have production and organisation capacity outside of the state sphere, has arisen: churches, NGOs, trade unions, brotherhoods, clubs and decentralised groups basically corresponding to middle-class interests. There has also been a return to identity seeking, especially around ethnic groups providing services that the state cannot take on. Violence occurs when the systems of inter-ethnic solidarity and balance break down.

Access to power has greater ascendancy over wealth than the inverse. Classes in the making are established on social status based on symbolic power and therefore on criteria other than economic position. Consequently it is difficult, despite levies, to assimilate the African peasantry into the exploited classes subject to "law of building on rock". This classic representation underestimates transfers, family strategies of human investment or the rural base of several parties in power (cf. the RDA and the PDCI of the Baoulé planters in the Ivory Coast). The *classes* that have economic capital (foreigners and national intermediaries) can be distinguished from the *intellectual elite* who possess educational capital (acquired through schooling), which is often in conflict with social and symbolic capital. Consequently, *social struggles* are not only about *class* (in the Marxist sense), but also about stature or *position* (for those holding cultural capital) and about "race" or ethnicity for those with social and symbolic capital. The post-colonial state is at risk against established coalitions built on power; it more often is a place where class is constituted than a reflection of class.

The *redistribution crisis* refers to a redefinition of the rules of the society. The middle classes (salaried employees, civil servants), whose salaries and guarantee of employment have disappeared, are expecting an illusionary return to the former redistributive model. Uprooted, urban informal workers have seen the removal of populist measures (e.g. food subsidies). Young graduates no longer have any hope of integration into the formal economy. The crisis enveloping the redistributive model is a sign of the discontinuity between modern production modes and the consumption model. The informal sector provides a means of controlling this crisis in the short term (Michailof 1993). Liberalisation has led to a growing gap between the aspiration towards a certain model of consumption and the exclusion of the largest number of people from this model. Declining income, the breakdown of public services and the integration into an international criminal economy have lead to a generalisation of petty crime, resulting in minimum income to employees, and major corruption, that has serious distortive effects. *Transparency International* ranks Nigeria and Cameroon first and second on the global list. A study by PNUD estimates its annual cost for Africa at close to $150 billion. Corruption leads to a relationship between corruptor and corruptee. Its effects are all the more negative, since almost all corrupted money is invested outside of Africa.

Chapter 6
Reproductive dynamics

For half a century, African behaviour has furthered a *demographic, urban, and educational explosion*. These have created costs that cannot easily be managed by the global economy, something that manifests today in an economic crisis, the questioning of intergenerational relations and a change in demographic behaviour. Institutional hierarchies based on age have been transformed. The urban model has been worn out by the hope of gains it has created, the city management methods it has brought about, and the education model that has failed since graduates can no longer hope for salaried employment in either the public or private sector. New forms of sociability but also of individualisation and exclusion are emerging. The *reproductive logic* is in a state of crisis and some prophets of doom look upon the demographic regulators of war, epidemics, and famines as impending risks.

6.1 Demographic growth

Belated demographic transition

Up from 210 million in 1960, Africa's population reached close to 700 million in 2000 and should be about 1,3 billion in 2025. The annual growth rate is close to three per cent; 20 per cent of the population is less than five years old; and 45 per cent younger than 15 years. There is a wide gap in the growth rate ranging from 2,3 per cent in southern Africa to 3,3 per cent in eastern Africa. The higher than three per cent average growth rate has only slightly decreased since 1995. The demographic explosion is, from a historic perspective, quite recent. Soon after the Second World War, African countries crossed the

TABLE 6: EVOLUTION OF THE AFRICAN POPULATION, IN MILLIONS (1960–2030)

	1960	*1990*	*2000*	*2030**
Sahel	16,7	36,5	46	100
Coastal West Africa	21,1	48,8	63,5	125
Nigeria	42,3	95,0	111,5	220
Central Africa	11,7	24,4	31,4	65
Great Lakes	20,9	48,3	65,6	126
(including the DRC)	(15,3)	(35,6)	(51,5)	(86)
Southern Africa	35,2	94,2	105,0	221
Indian Ocean	6,2	13,8	17,2	32
Eastern Africa	53,3	125,1	158,4	347
(including Ethiopia)	(24,2)	(49,2)	(63)	(159)
South Africa	17,4	35,3	41	65

* Forecasts for 2030 are highly uncertain especially on account of the Aids risk
Source: UN Statistics; FNUAP; African Development Bank 2000.

mortality threshold that took European countries more than 100 years to accomplish, whereas fertility rates remained high. Anti-mortality techniques spread long before antenatal techniques. *Demographic investment* expanded at the expense of economic investment that would have enabled increased productivity.

The artificial African *fertility* rate (on average 5,5 children per woman) can partly be explained by the economic value of children, as labour, old-age insurance, or a source of future transfers. Parents "invest" in children and the latter have redistribution obligations regarding their parents. Other explanatory factors include the high risk of mortality, memories of cataclysms and the demographic hole left in pre-colonial and colonial times, and the will to have an off-spring as an expression of the force to live. The gross birth rate (the relation between annual births and population size) has remained around 47 per cent for 30 years.

The issue of *mortality* necessitates reference to the differentiation between social classes, to macroeconomic variables and to external factors. There are significant inequalities regarding death between people from different social backgrounds and regions. The mortality rate remains high, although it has dropped significantly. The rate of 23 per cent in 1965 decreased to 15 per cent in 1990. Life expectancy has increased by almost 12 years since independence. Infant mortality dropped from 28,4 per cent at independence to 10,6 per cent in 1998.

Africa has belatedly broached its *demographic transition.* The drop in mortality, ongoing for more than half a century, has brought about only a belated drop in fertility. The effects of the demographic transition are more prevalent in cities and for women with primary and especially secondary education.

HIV/Aids has become the main cause of death, ahead of malaria, and has caused ten times more deaths than all wars on the continent. Africa has recorded 86 per cent of the world's deaths from the Aids virus (137 million people) and has 70 per cent of the world's infected population. Need one be reminded that 95 per cent of the money spent on Aids goes to five per cent of the affected population (Western countries) or that the cost of AZT treatment for the 4 million seropositive people in South Africa would be ten times its annual health budget? Southern Africa has been particularly affected. A third of the adult population of Botswana, a quarter of that of Swaziland, Zimbabwe and Lesotho, a fifth of that of South Africa, Zambia and Namibia, and a sixth of that of Malawi are infected with HIV/Aids. In 20 years time, life expectancy will have dropped by 26 years in Zimbabwe, from 65 to 39 years.

Besides the human drama (4 million orphans in Africa), HIV/Aids also has social and economic consequences. In particular, it contributes to the diminution of the elite; the active and most qualified population is severely affected. It is forecast that 25 per cent of civil servants in the Ivory Coast or 25 per cent of wage earners working for Eskom in South Africa will be seropositive. In western Africa, in the absence of HIV/Aids, the life expectancy would have been in the order of 59, that is to say, 16 years more than the current age.

The economic effects of the demographic explosion

This demographic explosion has a serious effect on an economy. Population statistics are pyramidal in shape with the base being the vast number of younger people. The rate of those that can be taught (percentage of population of school-going age) is two and a half times higher than in industrial countries; the dependency ratio (ratio between those that can be taught and the adult population) is around 0,5.

According to the Malthusian trap, demographic growth leads a system to its departure point, the subsistence minimum. In contrast, other authors such as Boserup and Hirschman defend the theory of *procreating pressures* and of African under-population (Amin 1976; Sautter 1990). There would be weak demographic density condemning societies to stagnation from the point of view of agricultural techniques if there were no increase in density. Most of the older works on Africa have shown that demographic density has been a factor in improving agricultural yield (Badouin 1979; Maldant et al. 1973).

Optimistic analyses combine the theories that agricultural production depends on urban demand, that technical innovation results from demographic pressure and that environmental conservation is a condition for sustainable agricultural development.

In Africa there is no significant correlation between demographic growth and economic growth. Demographic dynamics have progressive (or regressive) effects according to the system's capacity to adapt (or not) to a higher level. The major question is not as much about global overpopulation than about growth rhythms necessitating demographic investment that is borne with difficulty by the economy.

Most often, *ecosystems* do not have sufficient time to be restored. Firewood makes up half of all energy consumption. Deforestation results from land clearing, pastures for herds, energy needs and "raw" exports. It affects regions in the Sahel as well as the belt of forest cities (e.g. Kinshasa) or the high-density regions at high elevations (eastern Africa, Madagascar).

It is deemed that "the time of finite space is beginning" (Giri 1986). Available arable areas fell from 0,5 hectare units in 1965 to 0,3 hectare units in 1990, and was estimated to be around 0,2 hectares in 2000, the present levels in Rwanda or Somalia. *Demographic pressure* in conjunction with traditional techniques furthers environmental *degradation* (desertification, land clearing, soil erosion and the destruction of vegetation covering). This can be controlled only if accompanied by beneficial migratory flows and technical progress (29 countries will be in a critical situation in 2000 according to the hypothesis of weak utilisation of inputs). If it is necessary to control fertility, such control will have an effect only during the next generation.

6.2 Migration and urban explosion

African societies, currently in the process of becoming populated, are also in the process of remodelling their occupation of space. The number of *inter-African migrants* is estimated at 35 million. Historically sub-Saharan Africa, with some exceptions (e.g. the Senegal River valley or the Great Comoros valley), is characterised by large-scale emigration from Africa. Nonetheless, migrant transfers represent 80 per cent of Botswana's current deficit, 50 per cent of Lesotho's GNP or 70 per cent of Sudan's exports. The Ivory Coast in West Africa and South Africa in southern Africa are the two main centres of immigration. Africa is also the continent with the highest *refugee* workforce. The number of refugees assisted by the UNHCR, which was 950 000 in 1960, stood at 3,7 million in 1980 and close to 6,3 million (almost a third of the world total of 23 million) in 2000.

Internal migration is a permanent phenomenon in African societies. Colonisation generally modified these flows: the Arachidier basin in Senegal has thus become an area of immigration and of seasonal movement since the end of the 19th century. Since the Second World War, the crisis in rent-crop cultivation, added to demographic factors, has reoriented flows towards urban areas.

In some regions (e.g. the Mossi plateaux in the Great Comoros), migration is a means of perpetuating social structures. In contrast, in other regions (e.g. in Anjouan), the diversity of activities is a means of preventing migratory behaviour. Migratory flows are disrupted by rising nationalism, the establishment of property laws and the increasing scarcity of "free" land.

Urban growth

Most *urban growth* in Africa today is of a demographic nature and also stems from the territorial expansion of cities. The rate of urbanisation was less than ten per cent 30 years ago; in 2000 the average rate of urbanisation in sub-Saharan Africa was above 35 per cent. Western and eastern Africa are twice as urbanised as central Africa (20 per cent as opposed to 40 per cent). Megalopolises overlap without a genuine urban framework. There are large differences between countries: 95 per cent of Rwandan city dwellers live in Kigali as opposed to 21 per cent of Congolese city dwellers in Kinshasa. The decrease in the migratory balance from two per cent to one per cent a year, combined with a fall in natural growth from three per cent to 2,5 per cent a year, leads one to anticipate a fall in the urban growth rate from five per cent to 3,5 per cent.

There are many reasons for *migration.* According to Harris and Todaro (1970), the migrant compares the latest value of lost income flows with the latest value of urban incomes assumed likely; consequently all employment creation in the city increases migration. In fact, there are many determinants of individual migration and they cannot be reduced to behaviour based on a probability model. Family decision-making units arbitrate between rural and urban regions. Emigration regions are not generally the poorest ones. Migratory income helps to increase incomes from emigration areas. For the Serer and Diola of Senegal, migration is a matrimonial strategy.

The effects of urbanisation

The *effects of urbanisation* on economic development are complex. Migration can certainly enable a better human/land relationship, but history has not shown an optimal use of the land. There is no significant correlation between the urbanisation rate and per capita GDP growth. The "urban bias" (Lipton 1977) appears nevertheless to be limited. African *urbanisation,* which comes in various forms, generally does not lead to a severance of city/countryside linkages; urban agglomerations are linked to their rural *hinterland* and they have a flexible population. Urban agglomerations are places of intensified trade; the city is not only a place to offload agricultural surplus; it is also a wealth-creating space through the division of labour and the market, and a place of solvent demand. City consumption modes, especially of food, are diverse and non-uniform, as well as being superimposed, confrontational, and with their own dynamic (Cour 1992; Dubresson & Raison 1998; Requier-Desjardins 1989).

Thus, despite evidence to the contrary, the least urbanised countries in Africa are relatively the most food dependent, in the form of imports of food aid, and have the lowest rural agricultural added value (Hugon, Coussy & Sudrie 1989). Trade, stockpiling and transport networks are therefore an essential element of spatial connectedness.

The crisis in productive systems and *urban impoverishment* has nevertheless led to cities having a reduced effect on training and to an increase in youth unemployment. City and countryside are becoming reversible and are forming new links. Thus cities generally do not play a commanding role although they are poles of impetus. Young educated people are the agents fermenting the rural dynamic and connecting rural areas to cities. Africa's economic crisis has emphasised in particular the ruralisation and informalisation of African cities, and has greatly narrowed the gap between city and countryside (per capita urban added value was six times that of rural areas in 1980; this gap fell to only triple that in 1990). Owing to a lack of urban public management, demands for housing, transport, water, energy and sanitation are partly satisfied by popular initiatives, but urban ecosystems are deteriorating notably.

6.3 Human investment

The implosion of education

Education systems, like health systems, tended to develop very rapidly after independence. The high demand for education emanating from families, the desire of the authorities to reduce regional disparities and to make up for historical backlogs, to develop national educational capital and to Africanise jobs, and the weight of the demographic constraint are ultimately all factors that explain the "educational inflation" (Hugon et al. 1994). The educational machinery developed quickly according to its own logic and independent of socio-economic conditions. This resulted in a paradoxical situation.

Africa remains *undereducated* considering the size of its population. A third of all countries have a primary education rate below 50 per cent; four per cent have a gross secondary education rate below 15 per cent. Women, in particular, are excluded from education. During the 1980s, there was a tendency towards less education.

Africa is also *badly educated*. Quantitative expansion took place at the expense of quality education and at great cost. Most schools are in effect day-care centres rather than places of learning. The gap between places of learning for the elite and schools for the masses is increasing.

Africa is *over-educated* in relation to its financing capacity and employment structures. The elasticity of educational expenditure in relation to the GDP was higher than one for 20 years. Education expenditure is higher than four per cent of the GDP in two-thirds of all countries and makes up more than a quarter of current budgetary expenditure. Training costs are especially high. They amount to between 20 and 30 per cent of the per capita GNP for each pupil in primary education, 130 per cent for each pupil in secondary education, and 1000 per cent for each student in tertiary education. For the same rate of education, the relative financial outlay (in relation to the GDP) is almost ten times higher in Africa than it is in Europe.

The effects of human investment

Education certainly seems to be an investment and not only a consumer good. Its impact goes largely beyond that of training for productive work, salaried or non-salaried. It develops children's abilities, it has an effect on the birth rate, and it valorises a country's cultural inheritance and builds national identity. Education is an intergenerational investment, since the children's success depends on the family's educational background.

However, these different effects depend on the contents of training and on the production system. The school is only a vehicle for the knowledge that has been entrusted to it. The education system consists of different channels linked to the segmentation of the labour market (Vinokur 1994). The education of the social elite tends to happen outside of Africa.

Together with Hallak, one can talk about *educational "stagflation"*. Faced with the weak absorption capacity of school leavers by the economy, the educational explosion has led to a devaluing of graduates and to graduate unemployment, which has gradually started to affect higher levels, and leads to an exodus of skilled workers. The public and parastatal sector, the main employment provider during the first 20 years after independence, is cutting down on its workforce. The cost of creating a job in the modern private sector is higher than the salary life of a worker. The informal sector alone acts as a sponge, but does not require the knowledge acquired at school. Some econometric tests show that in Africa, training has not been a significant factor in growth (World Bank 1988) owing to the poverty trap.

PART THREE
ECONOMIC POLICIES AND PROSPECTS

Digging the well today will quench tomorrow's thirst (Peul proverb).

Nobody knows the story of the next dawn (Lobi proverb).

In hindsight, the African crisis is distinguished by three main instances of collapse: that of a post-colonial *trade economy* that specialised in primary products; that of a *managed economy* where the redistribution approach prevails, and that of *community economies* where production dynamics are vital. Hence the development of *liberalisation policies* (Chapter 7). These are driven from outside; they aim at introducing rationality into the allocation of resources and financial stabilisation. They are implemented by actors with their own rationality: they are at the heart of politics even though they wish to be apolitical, and thus have different effects according to the specific *direction* of each economy (Chapter 8). In a context where what is at stake for Africa and in Africa has already evolved, these policies lead to negative and differentiated medium-term *prospects* (Chapter 9).

Chapter 7
Subject to liberal policies?

7.1 The breakdown of interventionist policies

There appear to be five global factors responsible for the breakdown mentioned above. The *agro-export* model, based on selling tropical products to small markets and in the face of increasing competition, has tailed off. The *import substitution strategy* has limited validity in micro states where markets are stagnating and where protectionism is creating rents and reducing competitiveness. The *extensive agro-pastoral model* is based on the non-regeneration of ecosystems (shortening the period the land is left to lie fallow, deforestation, etc.). The state can no longer absorb young school leavers though the creation of *public and parastatal jobs*. It gives priority to *managing financial deficits*.

The *managed economy* put into place after independence was a substitute for the market; the state was the driving force of development; the tools for macro regulation relied on "Keynesian" instruments: budget, public investment, low interest rates, controlled prices, over-evaluation of the currency, and so on. It was assumed that the external constraints would neither weigh heavily, nor be undone by a voluntary withdrawal policy. Economic policies were selective and sectoral. Few African countries implemented central planning. On the other hand, intervention resulted from projects financed by external lenders according to criteria linked to referential prices (net social benefits of consumption) or the method of billing (additional national value expressed in foreign currency).

These policies had three foundations.

- According to the current *dependency*, Africa is part of a process of globalisation that is distorted and leads to internal dislocation (Babassana 1978; Bernstein & Campbell 1985; Bertrand

1975; Leys 1975). The integration into capitalism causes a stagnation in development through the taking over of the state apparatus by the bourgeoisie or the dependent classes. Consequently development implies a double break with the external world, with imperialism and with the "ruling classes", and embracing a "national and people's development path that could lead to socialism" (Amin 1976). This approach has been used in countries such as Ethiopia, Madagascar, Benin, Congo, Tanzania and now Zimbabwe.

- Intervention by the state as the main development actor is equally justified by a reformist *structuralist* approach. African economies are characterised by rigidities and bottlenecks. Consequently prices cannot respond to adjusting variables. Public powers have to intervene. It is a matter of implementing motivational sequences, of creating new comparative advantages: from the viewpoint of the Asian experience the "pro" state (promoter, producer, prospector, and programmer) has to play a key role. The state has to take account of externalities, returns to scale and indivisibility while also playing a stabilising and redistributing role. Lenders therefore support a mixed economy, or state capitalism.
- Finally, a *post-Keynesian* approach develops especially within the administration: the framework of national accounts, billing methods, instruments of interventionist policies, anticyclical budget policy, and stabilisation mechanisms.

Changes in the international environment, the escalation of the crisis, external debt, as well as internal financial imbalances linked to the rent-orientated economy have led to a radical change in policies under the impetus of the International Monetary Fund (IMF) and the World Bank.

7.2 Adjustment policies

Almost all African countries have implemented structural *adjustment* and *stabilisation* policies since the beginning of the 1980s.

Economic debates among donors

The *Washington* institutions, the IMF and World Bank, have played a pre-eminent role in the financial management of debt; in expertise; and in the control of information and modes of intervention, leading to the development of strategic frameworks. There is relative consensus among donors on the need for financial stabilisation, the removal of policy distortions, opening up towards the exterior, and institutional reforms leading to more democracy.

Nevertheless, there seem to be divergences on several points:

- The IMF and the French Treasury accord priority to *short-term* monetary and financial objectives, whereas the World Bank and the French Development Agency take a *medium-term* view.
- The Bretton Woods institutions follow a more *liberal* approach. The removal of protection should end rents, reduce financial costs, and lead to the emergence of efficient structures. The European Union and French co-operation traditionally was more in favour of a *gradual* approach and of a sliding protectionism to compensate for international asymmetries. Regional integration is thus seen as a precondition for opening up to the exterior.
- The *francophone notion* of development is more institutional and interventionist. It aims to put in place rules and institutions that will restore confidence, obliterate cheating, increase credibility, and therefore allow operators some degree of predictability. The *British approach* focusses more on a self-regulating market.

The liberal analysis of the African crisis

The crisis can be explained by the following, in order of priority:

- The *policy distortions* and the non-respect for true prices: real negative interest rates have promoted overcapitalisation and the selection of non-profitable projects. The low real prices paid to agricultural producers have not stimulated market supply. Controlled prices and administrative controls have prevented an optimal allocation of resources; they have promoted parallel markets. The over-evaluation of the exchange rate and control of external trade have prevented comparative advantages from being exploited; they have over-protected industries and discouraged the export sector. Institutional salaries do not reflect the surplus of labour.
- The *non-adjustment* or *late adjustments* to external shocks: during the 1980s Africa admittedly suffered from the effects of the deterioration in its terms of trade, but unlike the African continent, other continents increased their export volumes during the same decade. Bureaucratic rigidities prevented these adjustments.
- *Institutional shortcomings*: the quality of government has deteriorated (bureaucratic blockages, absence of transparency, *rent* seeking, weak judiciary system, arbitrary decision mak-

ing, etc.). Krueger, Bhagwati and Balassa liken the state to a collection of resources that allows a group to trade off the interests of its members over that of its clients. Civil servants have become a drain on the state.

Policy objectives

The economic policy instruments recommended by the IMF and World Bank, that is the "Washington Consensus", basically aim to ensure economic flexibility, to discontinue *rents*, and to assist in the emergence of innovative actors. The *stabilisation policy* aims, through exchange rate variation, to lower absorption and (or) ration money supply to reduce internal and external imbalances. *Structural adjustment* policies intend to achieve market and institutional reforms, allowing for the establishment of conditions for sustained growth.

Opening up to the world market rests on *the liberal principles of comparative advantage*, the *free circulation of factors of production and a balanced exchange rate*. The removal or relaxation of foreign exchange controls, the standardisation of real protection rates, approaching nominal protection, the removal of non-tariff protection (except for the rationing of some strategic products), and the readjustment of monetary parity should lead to a shift in the terms of trade and move productive sectors from protected towards competitive sectors.

More attractive *investment codes* are supposed to enhance capital entry and private initiatives. Opening up measures tend to reduce quantitative practices (controlled exchange rate, import quotas and licenses) and to approach the free trade market through allocating bids; they involve transparency in the allocation of foreign currency and making a percentage of foreign exchange available for imports and export companies. These measures are supposed to reduce or remove any backlog linked to controls, parallel currency markets, and "rents" linked to administrative controls. They further promote liquidity and profitability criteria at the expense of the effects of integration and remove any possibility for the state to juggle its priorities.

Internal liberalisation has to do with trade agencies, a reduction in the role of the state, the "slimming down" of public and parastatal enterprises, the dismantling of subsidies and stabilisation bodies, and the rationalisation and privatisation of the public sector. These measures should allow for much greater efficiency and remove the eviction effect of the public sector vis-à-vis the private sector.

The *reduction of absorption* (actual flow perspective) or of *internal credit* (monetarist perspective) should re-establish the external balance of payments equilibrium. This restructuring of demand is accompanied by loans that have been earmarked for the reconstruction of competitive sectors (structural adjustment and sectoral loans). The reduction of deficits, both budgetary and those of parastatal and state enterprises presupposes lower expenditures (deflation of human resources, removal of especially food subsidies, true to form/ actual public tariffs) and higher income (effects of devaluation, increase in especially oil taxes). Complementing the recovery from financial imbalance, *growth* should result from an increase in global public and private capital flows. Donor coordination and the globalisation of aid flows should allow, among other things, for the maintenance of a flow of positive transfers to each country (Assidon & Jacquemot 1988; Guillamont 1985; Hugon & Sudrie 1992).

Structural reforms

The most important aspect, however, lies in *structural measures*. Structural adjustment policies (SAPs) have gradually extended their temporal horizon and broadened their areas of intervention by integrating structures and political issues.

The first facet has to do with *deregulation and privatisation* measures; they aim to reduce waste, rationalise resources and find new, more efficient ways of management. The liquidation or dismantling of public agencies, the privatisation of public and parastatal enterprise management and/or capital, and the dismissal of public sector employees are measures aimed as much at reducing the eviction effects of the public sector as at creating subsidies for the modern private sector or the informal sector. To increase returns from public enterprises and reduce state intervention, provision has been made to settle arrears between the state and public enterprises, hold public enterprises responsible for the external debts they have contracted, liquidate inefficient enterprises or rehabilitate malfunctioning ones.

A second facet has to do with *institutional reforms*: they aim to improve management, achieve greater transparency, and have available information and coherent frameworks that will guide decision making.

7.3 Short-term policy inefficiency

African countries have undertaken serious reforms of their institutions and policies since 1980; this process was accelerated with the reinforcement of the structural adjustment facility during the 1990s. Loans, accompanied by favourable conditions, are subject to the implementation of a three-yearly reform programme. In November 1999 the Poverty Reduction and Growth Facility (PRGF) replaced the Structural Adjustment Reform Facilities (SARFs).

Since 1988, 27 African developing countries have launched a structural adjustment programme. There has been a rapid process of trade and financial liberalisation. With the exception of extreme positive or negative cases, real per capita GDP dropped by 1,4 per cent annually during the three years preceding these programmes and stagnated during the following three years, and dropped by 1,1 per cent during the three subsequent years (IMF estimate). The level of over-indebtedness has risen. Reforms have improved access to official financing, but have not impacted on private flows. Few countries have set in motion a "virtuous" cycle of debt reduction leading to more investment and exports, and in turn contributing to debt alleviation.

Stabilisation has been relatively successful (control of inflation, reduction of the budget deficit and the volume of debt, depreciation of the real exchange rate). The results are more uncertain and unequal in terms of structural reforms and sustainable growth. Apart from a J-curve as a result of the reforms, a certain lack of policy credibility and strong interests are neutralising the reforms. Policy success depends on the international and internal environment, as well as on the coherence of measures (*policy package*), the instruments used, the order of sequences and delays in their implementation.

Often-distorted policies

According to Guillaumont & Guillaumont (1994) adjustment has been informal, thwarted by the environment and shocks, myopic and borrowed. Countries that have undergone serious reforms have obtained the best results for macroeconomic stability. The per capita GDP has risen in only six of the 29 countries that have put in place serious reforms. Health and education provision indicators have tended to deteriorate. Export and imports have hardly increased in value and external payment deficits have remained high. The outflow of resources for debt servicing has reduced net transfers.

Some policies are inefficient in the degree to which economic stakeholders *anticipate* them. They are often diverted from their objectives. The authorities hardly accepted the imposed measures and saw loans as cash drawers.

Conceived within a national framework at different times and according to diverse sequences, adjustment programmes also came up against *interdependencies* between economies and national policies. Paradoxically they have thus then furthered informal channels (Coussy & Hugon 1991). SAPs have changed the rules of the game and have led to the emergence of new practices generally far removed from donor expectations.

Different, insufficient or negative effects

According to the proponents of adjustment measures, the expected *"virtuous" circle* is the following: adjustment loans linked to reform measures and financial stabilisation further the resumption of investment and productivity. This, in turn, leads to an increase in supply and external competitiveness, bringing about import substitution and a boosting of exports. The result is a rise in demand corresponding to the rise in supply.

In practice, the following *vicious circle* can often be observed: loans increase the importance of debt in the context of negotiable debt rescheduling and reimbursement of debt linked to loans. This results in reduced imports, investments and government expenditures, which bring about a drop in the volume of exports, and hence a decline in supply. In addition, the international context leads to price instability for exported primary products. This results in an inability to pay for debt servicing. Standing debt mechanisms require relaxed financial conditions (debt cancellation and reduction) that lead to non-project loans and allow positive financial transfers to be maintained (Hugon & Sudrie 1992).

Adjustment programmes have emphasised the *social dimension* (Cornia et al. 1987), the *environment*, institutional aspects, and "good governance". Sectoral adjustment loans, more than macroeconomic loans, have promoted the reconstitution of priority procedures/channels. Programmes have become less standardised and more tailored. Debt reductions have involved the Highly-Indebted Poor Countries.

Co-ordinating relationships with financiers and the putting in place of social networks have become the strategic frameworks for the struggle against poverty, taking into account the multidimentionality of the dilemma. Still, these frameworks are far from being on top of a lasting development, that would absorb exterior shocks, apathy, scientifical, technological and numerical fractures or the marginalisation that Africa is subjected to.

The removal of macroeconomic distortions is a positive gesture; the reduction of distortions seems to correlate with the resumption of growth, but there is an increase in external shocks, negative initial conditions or other passive factors.

Besides economic rationality, adjustment goes to the heart of politics, power games, and social compromises leading to *trompe l'œil* (illusionary) measures. The "political economy of adjustment" cannot be reduced to a utilitarian analysis of the state in terms of the interests of those who rule or to a functionalist analysis of the state. The patrimonial (Médard 1991) or rhizome state (Bayart 1989) feeds on the external world. Adjustment is at the heart of the arbitration between external credibility and internal legitimacy. This results in a "game of denial of failure" (Ferguson) in external relations. Donors keep recipients on a short leash, whereas rulers use cunning and present a façade in front of the Potemkin villages. The economic rationality of adjustment measures can therefore destroy the fragile socio-political balance and create a climate of insecurity, which has a negative retrospective effect on investment, according to Ferguson. The questioning of the "Washington consensus" has led to a greater linking of economics and politics, and to replacing *ex ante* conditionality in terms of modes with *ex post* criteria in terms of results.

Chapter 8
Diverse prospects

The *economic principles* of financial stabilisation and controlled opening-up policies are not debateable. The question is to know how these externally imposed policies fit in with the *prospects* of the diverse economies, how they are internalised or diverted by the practices of role-players, and according to which sequences they are implemented. One can distinguish three types of countries that existed in the 1990s (Collier & Gunning 1999): politically unstable countries with slow growth; politically stable countries with slow structural reform (growth of labour productivity about 2,7 per cent); countries with a healthy macroeconomic policy and stable political environment (growth of labour productivity 4,2 per cent).

As a consequence, it is necessary to open the "black box" of social structures, integrate *microeconomic behaviour* (cf. Part two) and reposition these macroeconomic policies by linking them to the *previous history* (cf. Part one). A typology therefore seems necessary. Africa is a diverse continent. Economic diversity seems to be favoured above the accumulation process, which hardly exists, and there are also specific "natural" or socio-political factors. *Accumulation regimes* linked to modes of *specialisation*, and *regional groupings* and *poles* linked to various dimensions will receive special attention as differentiating criteria.

8.1 Accumulation regimes and modes of specialisation

Four *accumulation regimes* can be distinguished according to international specialisation criteria. An accumulation regime provides the means of allocating any economic surplus to ensure appropriateness between production and consumption conditions over a long period. This regime corresponds to *institutional conventions* and mechanisms linked to the *production capacity of the economy* (cf. the French regulation school). This typology, of course, is reductionist. According to other criteria one can distinguish between transit or warehouse economies (e.g. Gambia, Togo, Benin), war economies (those of Ethiopia, Somalia), nomadic economies (the Touaregs), or landlocked economies (Sahel).

War economies

Between 1970 and 2002, Africa has been the theatre of 35 wars. Since 1990 (the end of the Cold War) the instrumentality of religion and ethnicity and the development of a criminal economy (drugs, diamonds, oil, weapon trafficking – the objectives and sinews of war) have increased conflict.

Some *war economies* have become areas of chaos: places of confrontation between warlords (Somalia, Chad); of ethnic conflicts (Liberia); of confrontation between gangs controlling smuggling routes (cf. the drug trade). These societies, disintegrating and living in anarchy, no longer have mechanisms to regulate either institutions or the state. The Horn of Africa (Somalia, Sudan) and other areas (Great Lakes, Congo, Ivory Coast) have been in turmoil since 1995. Stakes in oil and mining have encouraged or created conflicts (Angola, Congo, Gabon).

More than 20 per cent of the African population has been affected by civil wars or armed conflicts. The DRC is the epicentre of a zone of chaos and is still being looted. The risk of war is ever-present in western Africa (Liberia, Sierra Leone, Guinea and Ivory Coast) (Hugon 2001). Since the year 2000, the Ivory Coast has become a major obstacle in the termination of regional conflict.

Risks of war emerge when minority groups anticipate gaining more from war than from the sustainable distribution of rent income during times of peace (Azam 2000). At the same time, the increase in the number of conflict zones in Africa is the result of the exploitation of natural resources, ethnic nationalism, unemployment, the conscription of uneducated youths to reduce the cost of war activities, the dispersion of the population in uncontrolled territories, the failure of the rule of law and the seizure of power, the interference of regional and international powers, the globalisation of international criminal organisations and the role of diasporas (Collier & Hoeffler 2000; Hugon 2003).

Stationary economies

The structures of *stationary economies* closely resemble the colonial trade economy (cf. p.10) in that they are largely dependent on agro-pastoral activities and highly vulnerable in relation to the outside world. Some economies and regions such as the Cape Verde or the Comoros Islands, Burundi, Rwanda, the Palaeolithic mountains of the Sahel-Sudanese region are subject to *Malthusian demographic pressures*; others, such as the Central African Republic, Malawi or most of the countries in the Sahel suffer the inconvenience of being land-locked. In some countries that were well endowed with resources in the past, such as Uganda or Madagascar, *social structures* and *political factors* have played a determining role in blocking accumulation.

The economies in the *Sahel area* are very fragile. The Sahel is a relatively homogenous area from a climatic, pedological, demographic, social, or economic point of view. Peul nomadic pastoralists and Arab Berbers co-exist with sedentary livestock owners and Christian farmers. By and large, populations are not quite settled: urbanisation, limited before, has exploded. Export cultivation is limited to peanuts and cotton: the latter is the main source of monetary income for peasants and acts as a multiplier in rural settings. Some countries such as Mauritania or Niger also export mining products. Other countries, such as Chad, are becoming oil exporters with oil projects having doubled the state's budget.

These economies have to manage the double instability of the international (and regional) environment and of climatic hazards, whereas demographic pressures and public expenditures create costs that can scarcely be reduced. The main internal adjustment variables are the informalisation of the economy, internal and inter-African regional migration, and social networks that play a redistributing role. External aid, which finances the budget account and the current account balance, is a key adjustment variable.

Mining and oil economies

The specific dynamics of *mining* (Botswana: copper, diamonds, nickel; Guinea: bauxite; Liberia and Mauritania: iron; Niger: uranium; Sierra Leone and Togo: phosphates; DRC and Zambia: copper) or *oil* (Angola, Congo, Gabon, Nigeria) economies are centred on the creation and circulation of *rents* (strong state involvement, high investment rate, dominance of multinational companies, highly unstable income).

The development of these economies depends mainly on the prices of raw materials, the strategies of the mining companies, and policies that secure access to raw materials (e.g. the Elf group in the Congo or in Gabon; Shell in Nigeria; the Union Minière of upper Katanga in the former Zaire; the role of Anglo-American in South Africa). They have a very pronounced *dualist* structure. The mining sector, while generating budget income and foreign currency, mobilises the bulk of investment and finances imports. Mining cities are distribution poles that have a macroeconomic and regional effect.

The rest of such an economy is based on a precarious production apparatus and is strongly supported by an enlarged redistribution system. Mining income represents on average more than 90 per cent of exports and more than half the budget income. The state-centred economy financed with mining rent income is linked to a developed informal economy. The importance of the tertiary sector and the weakness of the agricultural sector are characteristic structural traits. These economies have suffered from the oil syndrome (Géronimi 1992) and, in several countries, from wars linked to diamonds or oil.

Oil rent should ease financial constraints. In the upstream industrialisation model, accumulation takes place around the petrochemical industry. In reality, spillover effects are limited owing to capital and consumer goods imports, profit and expatriate salary repatriation, and capital flight. The Congo's oil rent (eight million tonnes) accounts for nearly two-thirds of the budget income and 90 per cent of foreign currency. It is managed without any transparency through agreements between the state, Hydro Congo, and the oil companies, especially Elf. The latter provides 2,5 million inhabitants with the same funds as are available to a civil service of 85 000 people. A debt greater than US$1bn, as well as rent incomes, have been squandered through non-productive expenditures (e.g. the Northern Road) or been moved out of the Congo.

During a *boom* period, the increase in foreign currency-denominated income raises the value of the local currency and reduces the competitiveness of other export sectors while encouraging food imports. The prices in protected sectors rise; there is recourse to external finance; and highly capital-intensive investment creates an impoverishing effect.

During the *counter-shock* period, the economy experiences a combination of financial imbalances and the effects of recurrent cost and current expenditure inertia. Admittedly, state policies do modify these effects. For example, states stabilise rent incomes (the Cameroun placed such incomes on the international market); they finance infrastructure projects that would further the development of the agricultural sector (Niger) or smooth price variations (Botswana put 60 per cent of its diamond income into a stabilisation fund).

Agricultural exporting countries

Several countries that are *agricultural exporters*, thus benefiting from privileged access to external credit, have experienced an accumulation dynamic that exceeds the recently worn out import substitution model; this has been the case especially in the Ivory Coast, Kenya, and Ghana. This model has been based on the protection of consumer industries, the requirement of external capital and managerial staff, and a product market reserved for a Westernised elite. These countries, lacking mining wealth and oil reserves, have based their development on the export agriculture sector (coffee, tea, cattle breeding in Kenya; cocoa, coffee, palm products in the Ivory Coast; cocoa and coffee in Ghana). Thus, shortly after independence, the Ivory Coast put in place an accumulation model *dependent on state regulation* and based on the immigration of labourers (mostly the Mossi from Burkina Faso), European expatriate managers and capital inflows.

The importing of these production factors, linked to the availability of land, led to a specialisation in agricultural export products and the development of a dynamic modern industrial sector. This model, after going through a serious crisis owing to a combination of sliding prices and an unmanageable external debt, experienced a revival from 1994 to 1998 and then again faced a serious crisis from 1999 to 2003, which was linked to socio-political adjustments, a fall in prices, and other factors such as civil war in the Ivory Coast.

Industrial economies open to the outside world

There are some cases, especially in southern Africa and in the Indian Ocean Rim (Mauritius), of *accumulation in an open economy* linked to political stability.

The *Zimbabwean* economy in the 1980s (Grégoire 1989) was marked by political stability and relative prosperity. An agricultural storehouse with a good infrastructure, a high level of research and training, and abundant natural resources, Zimbabwe experienced significant industrial progress despite being landlocked. The economy was based on a dynamic African "communal sector" and a European capitalist sector. Industry accounted for 40 per cent of the GDP. Nevertheless, Zimbabwe is still marked by climatic hazards (cf. the 1992 and 2002 drought), the risk of ethnic conflict and populist policy. Hyperinflation and a fast depreciating currency are having a devastating effect on the Zimbabwean economy.

Botswana, a landlocked country, experiences high economic growth due to its making good use of its natural resources (especially diamonds) and spillover effects from South Africa (supplying 80 per cent of imports), as well as a liberal policy with regard to capital, combined with the stabilisation of export income. Diamond resources have created budget and current account surpluses and have allowed for the financing of infrastructure and social services. Education and health expenditures increased by 170 per cent between 1980 and 1998.

The 1980 ratio of aid to GDP of seven per cent fell to two per cent in 1998 (as against seven per cent and 15 per cent respectively for developing countries). Botswana, the only country to have left that club, has put in place an aid planning and management system. Its literacy rate of 41 per cent in 1970 rose to 79 per cent in 1999. On the other hand, it is the country with the highest rate of HIV/Aids infection (a third of active adults). Life expectancy, which increased from 55,5 years in 1971 to 65,3 years in 1991, had fallen to 46,2 years in 2000. It is estimated that the GDP growth rate will be reduced by a third as a result of the pandemic in the course of the next few years.

The effect of *economic policies* therefore differs according to the specific trends of different economies.

8.2 Regional integration

Adjustment policies conceived within a national framework also come up against the issue of *interdependence* between economies, while at the same time calling into question *regional integration and cooperation*. The weakness of institutional integration is in stark contrast to the intensity of unofficial liaisons (Coussy & Hugon 1991). Porous borders lead to "de facto free trade areas" (Giri 1986). Landlocked countries are de facto *integrated*. At least there are potential unifying poles. Small countries act as *entrepôt* or transit areas (Benin, Gambia).

The failure of institutional integration

After independence it seemed as if the "Balkanisation" of Africa was a factor causing external vulnerability, limiting internal growth possibilities and reducing its influence in international negotiations. The narrowness of national markets diminished the operation of economies of scale. The lack of national policy coordination has led to the duplication of non-viable competing projects. Since the 1960s, therefore, various regional bodies have been established (there were more than 200 in 1990, of which more than 80 per cent were intergovernmental bodies) and different forms of inter-African relations, of regional cooperation and integration have appeared

Mauritius

In 20 years *Mauritius* has moved from the mono-cultivation of sugar to a diversified economy resembling the newly industrialised Asian countries. It was able to adjust its growth and *devalue competitively* during the second half of the 1980s. Its economic success results from a combination of several factors such as the importance of tourist income, the existence of dynamic export trade networks, the success of the industrial free zone, the long existence of a qualified low-wage workforce, the state's capacity to ensure financial stabilisation, or the stabilising role of the sugar protocol with the EU. The dynamism of the private sector has allowed it to convert sugar rent income into industrial investment. Unlike South Korea or Taiwan, the state has not been the driving force; external protection has nevertheless played an important role. While taking account of wage increases (in 1992 the wage gap between Madagascar and Mauritius was one to eight), the economy is ensuring the recovery of different sectors, especially in upmarket textile products and export diversification (food, jewellery, electric and electronic products).

The product growth rate was nearly eight per cent during the 1980s. Per capita income rose to US$3000 in 1996. The budget deficit was two per cent of the GDP. Mauritius was able to attract private capital, especially from South Africa and Hong Kong. It has created an *offshore* banking sector. The free zone comprises 600 enterprises offering 100 000 jobs and full employment is ensured even though Mauritius has undergone demographic transition.

The island is nevertheless experiencing serious problems, especially of an ecological nature. It also has to rise to the challenge of the disappearance of the sugar protocol and the Multi-Fibre Arrangement (MFA). ❐

(World Bank 1989; Coussy & Hugon 1991; Diouf 1986; Ouali 1990; Robson 1987; Schulders 1990; Hugon 2001; African Development Bank 2003).

The *results* of *de jure* integration are limited, as far as trade (less than six per cent of total trade) and financial flows are concerned. With the exception of monetary unions, there is weak coordination of national economic policies. Numerous regional sectoral projects have failed. Nevertheless, there are potential complementaries. On the other hand, one can observe significant "informal" flows based on cross-border trader networks. The latter perpetuate trading traditions based on social solidarity and pre-colonial networks. More fundamentally, numerous peripheral economies tend to be structured around accumulation centres or unifying poles such as South Africa.

Regional integration nevertheless seems to be a *popular idea* and a reality, especially with the transformation of the OAU into the African Union and NEPAD initiatives. This has translated into multiple projects. Faced with the rise in regional blocs, the African Union and NEPAD aim to increase Africa's negotiating capacity. This organisation can increase credibility and restore the confidence of operators. It allows for the coordination of economic policies and can render adjustment more efficient. It is a way of opening up economies to the outside world at an acceptable pace. It can also reduce conflicts.

8.3 Regional poles or powers

Finally, policies have different effects according to the size of the countries. There are several *regional poles*: South Africa within southern Africa; Nigeria within West Africa; and the monetary unions within the franc zone that can act as a potential counterbalance.

South Africa[1]

South Africa, with 1,2 million square kilometres for 43,5 million inhabitants and a GDP of US$113,3bn (2001), is the dominant power in Africa south of the Sahara. The Republic of South Africa accounts for 30 per cent of exports of the nine most important minerals in the

1 In 2002 South Africa's real GDP increased by 3,1 per cent as against three per cent in 2001 owing to growth in the agricultural and manufacturing sectors and in platinum production (main export item followed by gold and diamonds). On the other hand, the value of the rand dropped by 37 per cent in 2001, but recovered most of those losses during 2002 and early 2003.

world. In sub-Saharan Africa, it accounts for 50 per cent of waged employment, half of the railway network, 40 per cent of the road network, and 50 per cent of energy consumption. The agro-pastoral sector, which groups together nearly 13 per cent of the economically active population, contributes up to 4,2 per cent of the GDP and is leading to alimentary self-sufficiency. The mining sector, employing eight per cent of the economically active population, contributes to 7,5 per cent of the GDP. Manufacturing industries (basically import substitution), employing 16 per cent of the economically active population, have a 20 per cent share in the GDP. South Africa is also a military power (military expenditures account for nearly ten per cent of the GNP). As a country that has been protected for a long time, where five conglomerates control a large slice of the economy and where the state has played a central role, South Africa is currently undergoing serious transformation.

Disparities remain high. Although the average per capita GNP in 2001 was around US$3000 (US$9500 in PPP), it varied drastically between whites, blacks, Indians, and coloureds; 80 per cent of arable land belongs to whites (12 per cent of the population). Unemployment and underemployment affect more than half of the population. GDP growth is low and foreign investment remains limited (15,6 % in 2001).

The South African growth model has experienced a systemic crisis for several decades. Its foundations raised questions, be it mining rents, the previous exploitation of black labour or state intervention in import-substitution policies (Cling 2000). The economy was stagnating. It is being liberalised and is moving from "growth through redistribution" to redistribution through growth; the opening up to the exterior is leading to a necessary change in specialisation.

South Africa remains to some extent a mining economy caught in a stranglehold by the gradual exhaustion of its precious mineral reserves. With relations with 43 African countries, South Africa largely dominates the economies of southern African countries. The collapse of *apartheid*, the end of the Cold War in Africa, the weight of conglomerates, the liberalisation taking place within the SADC, and the free trade agreement with the European Union are all factors encouraging its role as the integrating pole of southern African economies. The end of *apartheid* has led to high costs in integrating the communities. The main uncertainties are centrifugal tendencies linked to regional disparities, the rise in unemployed black youth (40 per cent of graduates), white and coloured fears in the face of violent crime, and *affirmative action*. The burning questions concern the reconciliation of the redistribution of power and wealth, and the implementation of an efficient productive system with the nec-

TABLE 7: COMPARISON BETWEEN THE CFA IN THE FRANC ZONE AND THE CFA IN SUB-SAHARAN AFRICA OUTSIDE OF THE FRANC ZONE (1975–1997)

	Franc zone			Outside the franc zone		
	1975–1985	1986–1993	1994–1997	1975–1985	1986–1993	1994–1997
Real growth rate of the GDP (% of annual average)	4,6	0,1	5	1,4	2,5	4,6
Real growth rate of the GDP/ inhabitant (% of annual average)	1,7	–2,8	2	–1,3	–0,3	1,7
Rate of inflation (% of annual average)	11,2	1,1	12	17,8	22	–
Budget balance (average % of GDP)	–5,0	–7,6	–1,5	–6,1	–5,6	–
Running exterior costs (average % of GDP)	–6,5	–7,4	–5	–1,9	–0,8	–
Exportation of merchandise (average % of GDP)	28,0	22,3	22	20,7	24	34
Importation of merchandise (average % of GDP)	23,8	18,7	29	18,9	20,9	33
Exterior debt (average % of GDP)	38,2	73,7	110	25,2	57	70

Source: IMF, *Perspectives économiques mondiales*, 1997; (Hugon, 1999).

essary external credibility for the "African Renaissance". How to safeguard a protected industrial sector faced with liberalisation? How to reconcile the support of powerful trade unions for job and salary protection with liberal macroeconomic policies attractive to capital and the necessary improvement of competitiveness?

Nigeria

Nigeria is the second largest power in sub-Saharan Africa. The sixth largest exporter of oil in the world, an OPEC member, integrated within ECOWAS, a market of nearly US$100bn in 1980, but only US$44bn in 1999, Nigeria is the *dominant economic power* in West Africa. A federal state, it accounts for about one-sixth of the continent's population (more than 110 million people), nearly 20 per cent of the GNP and 40 per cent of the external trade of sub-Saharan Africa. It has great potential. It has large reserves of natural energy (oil, gas), and agricultural, water, and mining (iron, columbite) resources. The road, banking and commercial infrastructure is developed and educational facilities have allowed for the formation of a high-level elite. In a society that attributes great value to money, there is a traditional trading spirit, and it has been equally able to link to international capital and to be manifest in the "informal sector" which covers all activities. However, Nigeria remains a "giant with clay feet"; it combines ethnic and regional differences and serious income inequalities with unstable oil resources. It is in effect a single product exporter, with growth regime fluctuations according to the oil situation: the economy shows many of the symptoms of the *oil syndrome* (Hugon in De Bandt & Hugon 1988).

The Nigerian economy faces serious *bottlenecks* that include the lack of managerial and technical skills, the importance of tribalism in the allocation of jobs, political criteria in locating industries, a bloated administrative apparatus, the low profitability of large projects (e.g. the steelworks in Ajaokuta), and poor electrical and other services. The establishment of productive units does not seem to have created an autonomous dynamic in the productive system; the latter, highly dependent on external influences, is characterised by technical, financial and management malfunctioning.

The *adjustment programme*, which was started in 1986, revolved mainly around foreign exchange liberalisation and the successive devaluation of the naira, price changes, the abolition of *marketing boards*, and monetary and fiscal policy control. A drop in overall internal demand, the gap between foreign exchange rates on the official and parallel markets, and the CFA franc's convertibility premium, linked to the effect of the size of the Nigerian economy with regard to neighbouring micro nations, have led to the conquest of regional markets and the reversal of trade flows between Nigeria and bordering countries. On the other hand, in 2000 Nigeria was not industrially competitive on international markets.

The franc zone countries

The *franc zone* arose as an preventative measure after a serious crisis (Gerardin 1989; Guillaumont & Guillaumont 1988; Hugon 1999). Officially created in 1948 between France and its colonies and protectorates, it has grown from a forced monetary integration to monetary co-operation between France and 15 African countries: the latter, with the exception of the Comoros, are grouped into two monetary unions each with a central bank. Free transferability means that France guarantees the convertibility of the CFA (African Financial Community) franc to a fixed exchange rate in relation to the euro, based on transaction accounting mechanism rules concerning monetary policy.

The existence of a common *monetary unit* and disposition imposes a certain discipline: it encourages compensation between countries and allows for the absorption of short-term shocks; but it can also delay and/or reduce adjustment in the case of long-lasting shocks. A *fixed exchange rate* creates a nominal anchoring point favourable to economic policies, limits foreign exchange risks and encourages community discipline; but it reduces flexibility and leads to adjustment in real terms. *External convertibility* furthers capital mobility and trade, but can also lead to capital flight linked to trade with countries with inconvertible currencies. The CFA franc has been retained to benefit from its convertibility premium.

During the *first two decades* of independence, African countries in the franc zone experienced greater exchange rate stability, as well as better economic performance as far as external trade and growth were concerned, when compared to other African countries outside the franc zone (Guillamont 1988). The state's current account deficit, as well as the inflation rate, has been further reduced. On the other hand, one sees larger public enterprise deficits, as well as increasing recourse to external financing. Several malfunctions appeared, however, for internal reasons such as disregard for rules, adjustment delays, and over-costing leading to a loss of competitiveness, or owing to external causes such as cumulative devaluation and capital flight from countries with inconvertible currencies, and anticipation of devaluation.

In a context of *real term adjustment* without devaluation, high interest rates, necessary for attracting capital, and the absence of monetary financing of budget deficits were emphasised.

The devaluation of the CFA franc in January 1994 led to significant economic progress in a favourable international context. The financial and macroeconomic effects of the CFA franc devaluation conformed overall to expectations. The GDP stagnated in 1994, then increased from 1995 to 1999 by around five per cent a year. The balance of payments surplus increased and the net position of the transaction account with the French Treasury improved by FF11bn in 1994. The inflation rate returned to five per cent after two years.

On the other hand, the structural questions of low investment and insufficient competitiveness remained; the Ivory Coast is experiencing a crisis, aggravated by the civil war, and is still awaiting the investments that would bring about a change in international specialisation and industrial structure. An institutional environment to promote productive investment does not exist.

Devaluation and adjustment have created an opportunity for a change in specialisation and for making the economy more flexible and competitive. The CFA countries still specialise in "commodities" with low income elasticities, very unstable prices and limited market prospects. The rent income from devaluation may assist in constructing new comparative advantages and in having a positive positioning on the global market.

Devaluation was accompanied by the creation of a customs and economic union within WAEMU and the CEMAC, with the former showing more satisfying results.

The destiny of the franc zone comes to the fore again in the new context of the euro. Monetary reforms will only be meaningful if they encourage capital entry, and if Europe exercises the contagion effects of growth through technology transfers and by opening up its market to manufactured products that would allow for an increase in the range of African exports (Hugon 1999).

In 2004, in contrast to areas of chaos (Great Lakes, Ivory Coast, Liberia), evidence of an "African Renaissance" could be seen in CEMAC, in eastern Africa and in southern Africa. The prospects of the African economies are affected by the global context (trade multilateralism, financial globalisation) and the European context (Cotonou Agreement based on free trade areas, aid fatigue, establishment of the euro, etc.). They are also affected by external shocks (climate, terms of trade) and internal conflicts.

Chapter 9
Issues and prospects

Since the fall of the Berlin Wall, Europe's direction, indeed its capital flow, has tended to turn towards Eastern Europe. In the eye of the media, Africa seems to be a place of *dramas*, of wars, epidemics, and famines. Seen from the inside, Africa, where some winds of democracy are blowing, is undergoing a profound *transformation*. This altered focus also provides an opportunity for Africans to become responsible for their own development.

9.1 Africa's interest

Africa is no longer a stake in the intense ideological bid as it was during the Cold War. However, that does not mean an end to diplomatic rivalries and factional struggles supported by foreign powers. The rise in *tensions* and *conflicts* is much more significant given that there is less economic interest in conquering markets than in capturing natural resources (e.g. diamonds or oil) and in controlling illicit trade (smuggling, drugs, etc.). In societies where the nation-state is still under construction and where personal networks and ethnic solidarity prevail over the institutionalisation of the state, the economic crisis has reinforced the dismantling of the state. In some extreme cases it has transformed the rent-orientated economy into a Mafioso and plundering economy. Consequently, the future of the economy is conditional to the future of the state.

From aid to economic interference

With the exception of oil and forward-looking mining interests, Africa is no longer of strategic interest because of the risk of chaos.

The countries in the "zone of influence" are integrated into the Priority Zone of Solidarity (PZS). Africa holds less economic than cultural interest in the context of permanent indebtedness. Foreign aid appears to be on a drip, allowing the state to assume a minimum of governing functions, but translating into increasing interference.

Interference is of an *economic* nature, with conditionality linking loans to economic policy choices and performance criteria. Budgets are interfered with as soon as the Washington authorities set up public investment programmes. Imports are also affected through the allocation of unrequited funds, as is the hard core of social expenditure. In several sectors one notes a return of expatriates, and privatisation most often leads to denationalisation. Interference is also of a *political* nature as soon as conditionality has to do with democracy. The international community has become more interventionist in the face of rising tensions: ethnic and border conflicts, migratory risks, natural catastrophes, and a rise in Muslim fundamentalism. Western public opinion and the United Nations support humanitarian intervention where doctors and those who distribute provisions are backed up by military forces. The traders, military forces and missionaries of the colonial period are reappearing, only, doctors have taken the place of missionaries.

9.2 What economic policies?

Economic policies have to be specific owing to a diversity of systems. Some *general principles* have to be re-established. Before there can be an in-depth restructuring of the economy, the priorities seem to be the restoring of confidence, rebuilding of a favourable *institutional context* and establishing the rule of law leading to legitimate power and allowing investment to return.

There certainly are economic debates internal to Africa, but Africa is more of a spectator than an actor. States no longer have either the analytical capacity or the information systems that enable them to establish long-term strategic frameworks.

On the other hand, there seem to be many *transformations*. "The dynamics expressed in contemporary Africa are often a sign of anomy but certainly not of lifelessness" (Raison 1984). The rising classes are criticising rent orientation, the personalised relations of clientilism and wasted, diverted, and distorted aid. Internal demands for democracy are leading to more transparent actions as illustrated by national conferences. States that often stray from performing their functions, where there is no distinction between the administration and politics, and where the association of public affairs with private patrimonies is a sign of corrupt practices, are again being questioned.

Towards a mixed economy?

Economic policy is an institutionalised compromise that cannot correspond to an ideal order albeit liberal or voluntarist. African societies are characterised by an *overlapping* of positions of *power* and *enrichment*, and a fluidity between the public and the private, forcing one to question again the opposition between state and market or the public and private sectors. In Senegal, the Mourides religious brotherhood, which is linked to the state, controls the peanut trade. In the Comoros, four families, close to the state, control all imports and exports. In West Africa, the Lebanese, and in eastern Africa and the Indian Ocean, Indians, act as the state's financiers in return for benefits received. Liberalisation and privatisation have generally transformed rents linked to state control into private monopoly rents.

The market cannot function without a "caretaker" or a proper organisation for several reasons. Global prices are not in equilibrium. When prices are unstable and uncertain, stakeholders, with their aversion to risk, have an interest in diversifying their production. Specialisation may be impoverishing since false information is circulated and since export growth leads to lower prices. True prices lead to a downgrading of part of Africa's agricultural and industrial productive apparatus. Consequently, one has to take into account conversion possibilities and the costs attached to the loss of learning related to this downgrading. The dismantling of sectors when there is a downward swing in the economy makes it impossible to reconstruct them when there is an upward swing. Stabilising mechanisms are necessary to smooth fluctuations and take time lapses into account.

On the other hand, the *controlled economy* is a source of *rent* income, but stifles innovation. It cannot integrate the necessary flexibility and adjustment to the international market and technological changes. Experience teaches that overtaxing agriculture penalises growth, that high protection creates *rent* income and that market distortions have negative effects on resource allocation. The controlled opening of markets and competitiveness are necessary to stimulate investment and an increase in productivity. The optimal allocation of scarce resources is obviously necessary.

Consequently, it is a matter of regulating the market and putting in place a *mixed economy* where the state creates a strategic framework and encourages a private entrepreneurial dynamic. The Asian "model" is largely based on, or has been based on, a subsidised export sector; an industrial sector destined for the protected internal market; a highly flexible productive system; and internal liberalisation allowing for the setting up of a true market driven by a strong state. The market is self-constructing and self-organising. Efficient enterprises need stable relations. Institutional changes are necessary. An incentive policy assumes that individual and collective apprenticeships will adopt new behaviours (Quiers-Valette 1994). The optimal reform sequence implies 1) economic stabilisation; 2) liberalisation of real national activities; 3) financial liberalisation; 4) external trade and capital liberalisation. Reforms have to reconcile the time necessary for learning and the necessity to end dependence on rents through radical reforms.

The Asian example has shown that it may be necessary to protect infant industries and improve interest rates and that this may not have disincentive effects on exports. The resumption of risk-prone investments, capital repatriation and the extension of agents' horizons presupposes a reassuring institutional framework and stable and legitimate political regimes.

The constitutional state, as opposed to special regimes, has to be accompanied by the easing of controls and a juridical framework. Economic agents need stable rules: land ownership laws allowing for more intense cultivation and non-renewable resource management, social laws preventing the "exploitation" of dependants, and respect of trade and customs rules to prevent unfair competition. But formal legislation is at odds with feasibility and practice. "Customary" laws have to be interpreted according to the situation, according to judicial precedence. Neither sole individual ownership, which is exclusive, nor community ownership, which presupposes coercive discipline and a crushing of initiative, is favoured when managing many different laws (Lebris et al. 1982).

9.3 What perspectives?

African societies will have to manage the doubling of their population and the quadrupling of their urban population between now and 2030. They have to rebuild their ecosystems, make the collective and productive investments necessary for growth, and reposition themselves positively in the international division of labour. These different *challenges* imply *productivity increases* and *accumulation over the long-term*. What should one think about *African prospects* beyond adjustment? If one takes account of past trends, important foreseeable factors and policy choices, then several projections are conceivable. A *catastrophe scenario* can result from national or regional cataclysms, the exacerbation of civil wars, and the destruction of ecosystems. This scenario looms in zones of chaos, these being Liberia, Somalia, and the Great Lakes. However, there also seem to be less pessimistic prospects.

The crisis can translate into an opening of trading transactions; this approach is based on the diffusion of technical means that simultaneously promote innovation and social and spatial differentiation. An Africa of contrasts is captured in the globalisation of images, in the technical revolution and in reinterpreted tradition.

Crisis, breakdown and transformation have thus emphasised the ambiguity of an *Africa of contrasts*. It is difficult to discern events that will construct the future "which move(s) forward at a snail's pace" and significant phenomena that enable one to sketch paths that may become history. In retrospect, a few decades ago there was a prevailing pessimism about Asia owing to its social and cultural particularities. Development, nevertheless, happens over generations.

There will probably be an increasing *differentiation* among African economies. The agro-pastoral priorities of the Touareg nomadic economies are not the same for the gatherers of the equatorial forest or for the peasants of the Madagascar highlands. Choosing between an open- or inward-oriented economy is different for small coastal countries and for large countries. The terms of managing self-sufficiency and food security differ radically between small, overpopulated islands and large countries with an abundance of land. The South African and Nigerian growth poles in all likelihood play a very important role. Monetary unions in the franc zone can constitute a counterbalance or, to the contrary, break up and encourage the free-rider strategies of small member countries. Differences become more pronounced according to accumulation regimes and modes of specialisation. The landlocked Sahel countries and countries at war risk being marginalised. The agricultural exporting countries will experience impoverishing specialisation if they do not diversify their exports. Oil or mining rent-orientated countries will suffer great instability linked to rent fluctuations. Water will be a major issue.

Africa will have to confront the winds of global competition in a world where preferences are disappearing. However, it can only develop from its internal foundations (energising the endogenous economy, reducing the cost of basic goods and services) moving towards a widened market (Engelhardt 1998; Hugon & Sudrie 2000).

NEPAD (New Partnership for Africa's Development), adopted by the African Union in 2001, is an endogenous African initiative that proposes partnership, an African peer review mechanism, regulation of regional dimensions of strategy, governance and the role of the private sector. The main objectives are peace and security, sound governance, promotion of health and education, economic growth and investment. The ambitious objectives include an economic growth rate of seven per cent and US$60bn of annual investment. This top-down process, managed by five states, can be progressively appropriated for the other states and civil society. NEPAD raises questions relating to the issue of financing or appropriation by the people and its manipulation by some states or the international community. It constitutes a new (perhaps last) chance for Africa.

The Cotonou Agreement (2000), successor to the Lomé Convention, illustrates the loss of the special relations between the European Union and the ACP countries. In conformity with the World Trade Organization (WTO) it continues the trend towards the abolition of preferences. Compensatory mechanisms for agricultural (Stabex) and mining (Sysmin) product instabilities have disappeared. LDCs and non-LDCs are will henceforth be treated differently. Economic partnership agreements (EPAs), be they with countries or with regions (CEMAC, EAC, WAEMU, ECOWAS, SADC) are planned. Reciprocal free trade agreements will have high costs in terms of public income, and income from exports and imports. It is doubtful whether between now and 2020, when the EPAs will come into force, African countries will be able to put in place the necessary reforms. Of course, respect for the rule of law, policy lock-in, and the transfer of credibility from Europe are to be supported, but ways to attract private capital flows, which are currently highly problematic, need to be revived. In Africa there is a high risk of backsliding and divergence.

Conclusion

The introduction posed the question regarding the legitimacy of economic analysis in understanding Africa. Micro and macro tools have been used, but have also been questioned with regard to the "black boxes" of social structures, power relations and historical trends. The economy functions at two levels: formal structures that have some external legitimacy, and real structures, which reflect socio-political compromises and the accumulation of relational or social capital (Hugon 1968).

A productive and competitive economy implies the mobilisation of national and foreign skills (especially of the South) and the emergence of entrepreneurs, owing to the market and liberalisation measures. However, productive investment cannot take place without a favourable institutional framework, a facilitator state and a climate of confidence. Cross-border trade networks and informal dynamics can be mobilised, but they also have to be channelled if one wishes for financial and trade accumulation to lead to productive accumulation. These economic and political reforms also imply new international relations and, especially, a purging of debt that is not incurred at the expense of financial transfers to Africa. The latter has to regain credibility capital, which also depends on opinion makers and the stability of rules, to reduce uncertainty. Africa's current challenges can be taken up only through both *international and domestic* action.

It is important to remember the rough estimates that illustrate *international asymmetries*. The subsidies given to farmers in the North (more than US$360bn a year) are more than ten times higher than aid flow received by Africa, and this is 15 times lower than the aid received in East Germany before reunification. If one takes capital flight into account, it is estimated that the total debt of some countries, such as the former Zaire, equals the assets that have been put into European banks by beneficiaries of the system. The number of foreign experts in Africa almost equals the number of expatriate Africans in Europe. In fact, the total cost of 700 experts in Madagascar (including living and travelling expenses) is roughly the same as the salaries earned by 100 000 Malagasy civil servants. In an international context of asymmetrical liberalisation, the per capita income gap between Africa and Europe has doubled since independence and currently stands at 150:1.

The priority is to transform the international structure, so that preference can be given to creating equal opportunities, stabilising the economy, regulating criminal networks and putting in place a system of co-operative multilateralism. These challenges cannot be taken up without serious *internal reforms*: development is the result of the contradictory practices of agents, but also of long-term strategies. History shows that there are many routes to development. The history of the past 40 years has shown the inadequacy of imported models, be they linked to the ideology of participation of rural agents, the Marxist-Leninist outline of central planners, the development operations of engineers, or recently, liberal theories.

Society has many and asymmetrical decision-making centres, each with its own space, ways, horizon and logic. Economic development presupposes that dominant actors have a long-term view, that they can take investment risks and leading macro decisions. It is also the result of the internal dynamics of micro enterprises and petty activities that make up the basic fabric.

Is it possible, at the end of this journey, to answer the question on the dominance of *Afro-pessimism*, both as a revelation of and a factor causing the crisis, asked at the beginning of the book? Of course Africa has experienced tragedies, wars, epidemics and famines. However, one has to put the media, which simultaneously expresses fear with regard to a powerful continent and commiseration vis-à-vis hunger, into perspective. Somalia or Rwanda is no more or less representative of Africa than Yugoslavia is of Europe. The theoretical economist who writes about Africa from afar tends to emphasise the loss of competitiveness, stalled growth and low investment. The practising economist present on the ground is struck by the creativity, by the initiative of people in an urban setting, and by the emergence of new organisations and an entrepreneurial spirit that escape accounting records. Naturally, the scale of present challenges raises scepticism about the concept of a self-organising society, but sustainable economic development seems illusory if it does not lean on these cultural and social anchorings. If there is disenchantment in the face of the illusions of independence and the failure of the modernisation project, African economies have their own historicity while also being open to the world. They therefore reflect specific prospects. These will only be viable if Africa also catches up with global technical revolutions.

There seem to be several priorities: re-legitimise the state to perform its collective and ruling functions, enlarge the market, allow efficient organisations to emerge by enabling learning and collective knowledge, find ways of coordination that simultaneously maintain the flexibility necessary for international advancement and a continuity of relations that enable investment and risk taking, and create a stable framework allowing for long-term anticipation.

The market economy can only function efficiently if the state is reinforced to create a favourable institutional environment, if enterprises have a long-term investment approach, and if redistribution mechanisms allow for social tensions to be regulated.

Decolonising the relations with Africa implies decolonising views and vocabulary, and not replacing remaining colonial structures in terms of communities, primitive mentalities and ethnicity with "quick-fix"-ideas concerning civil society, transparency or good governance.

When one is faced with weak consensus among the international community that questions the principle of non-reciprocity to compensate for asymmetries, or stabilising mechanisms for countries that are vulnerable to shocks, it has to be remembered that between the strong and the weak, freedom oppresses and the law emancipates. One needs to reverse the process in order to allow a levelling out, to encourage learning or to accept different rules of the game or to take account of handicaps when the race is against doped and slow runners. For want of a positive and managed integration into the world economy, Africa may become the backyard of Europe and disintegrate into a gangster world economy.

SOCIO-ECONOMIC INDICATORS OF 40 AFRICAN COUNTRIES
(more than one million inhabitants)

	HDI value	Population (millions)			Urban population (%)	Adult literacy rate (%)	Real per capita GDP ($)			GDP ($bn)	Annual per capita GNP growth rate (%)			External debt of GNP – $bn (%)		Annual inflation rate (%)		
	2002	1990	2000	2030	2000	1998	1990	1995	1998	2002	1965–1980	1998	2000	2002		1980–1989	1990–1998	2000
1. Sahel		**36,5**	**46,0**	**100**			–	–	**300**	**11,5**	–	–	**182,0**	**21**	–	–	–	–
Burkina Faso	0,325	9,0	12,0	23	17	22	207	259	240	2,2	1,7	1,7	–0,4	61,3	1,4	14,1	6,6	5,5
Mali	0,386	9,2	11,5	24	29	38	301	267	250	2,3	2,1	0,8	2,1	130,8	3,0	3,6	9,3	5,2
Mauritania	0,438	2,0	2,8	5	59	41	557	478	410	1,0	0,1	1,3	1,7	275,1	2,7	9,4	5,3	6,1
Niger	0,277	7,7	10,8	24	21	15	328	215	190	1,8	–2,5	–1,0	–3,2	89	1,6	3,4	6,8	6,1
Senegal	0,431	7,3	9,7	20	48	35	557	581	300	4,3	–0,5	2,9	78,7	3,4	7,3	5,6	5,4	–
2. West Africa		**48,8**	**63,5**	**125**			–	–	**380**	**21,5**	–	–	**194,4**	**41,8**	–			
Benin	0,420	4,6	6,4	11	43	38	394	362	380	2,1	0,3	1,8	3,1	74,4	1,6	1,9	10,1	8,7
Ivory Coast	0,428	12,0	15,0	37	44	44	1045	825	700	19,3	2,8	1,3	–4,9	140,9	27,0	3,1	8,7	7,2
Ghana	0,548	15,0	20,6	35	37	69	394	399	390	5,2	–0,8	1,5	1,3	132,2	6,8	43,6	25,6	28,4
Guinea	0,414	5,9	7,8	15	28	36	1103	594	540	3,0	1,3	2,0	–0,3	115,6	3,5	–	6,7	–
Liberia	–	2,6	3,6	6	46	51	–	–	–	–	0,5	–	–	–	–	18,3	–	–
Sierra Leone	0,275	4,2	5,0	10	37	31	432	150	140	0,67	0,7	–6,4	4,9	206,6	1,4	54,1	32,5	29,3
Togo	0,493	3,5	4,9	9	32	55	454	333	330	1,2	2,7	–1,4	3,5	120,1	1,5	5,1	8,8	8,5
3. Nigeria	**0,462**	**95,0**	**111,5**	**220**	**45**	**61.1**	**314**	**256**	**370**	**41,0**	–	**0,6**	**1,3**	**92,9**	**38,1**	**14,2**	**38,7**	**32,5**
A: **ECOWAS** 1+2+3		**180,3**	**221,0**	**485**			–	–	**300**	**74,0**	–	**0,5**	**136,5**	**100,9**	–			

SOCIO-ECONOMIC INDICATORS (continued)

	HDI value	Population (millions)			Urban population (%)	Adult literacy rate (%)	Real per capita GDP ($)			GDP ($bn)	Annual per capita GNP growth rate (%)			External debt of GNP – $bn (%)		Annual inflation rate (%)		
	2002	1990	2000	2030	2000	1998	1990	1995	1998	2002	1965–1980	1998	2000	2002		1980–1989	1990–1998	2000
4. Central Africa		**24,4**	**31,4**	**65**			–	–	**550**	**19,2**	–	**–2,4**	**117**	**22,5**	–			
Chad	0,365	5,7	7,8	14	24	39	176	230	230	1,4	–1,9	0,1	–2,1	79,9	1,1	1,5	8,3	8,1
Cameroon	0,512	11,8	15,3	33	49	73	730	646	610	8,8	2,44	–5,2	2,8	11,6	8,9	6,6	6,1	6,5
Congo	0,512	2,3	3,1	7	66	78	776	821	680	3,2	2,7	–1,3	4,9	219	7,0	0,3	7,1	9,2
Gabon	0,637	1,2	1,4	3	83	63	1678	3611	4170	4,9	5,6	0,5	–0,6	94,2	4,6	–1,0	7,2	5,7
Central Africa	0,375	3,0	3,8	7	42	44	417	–	300	1,1	0,8	–0,8	1,1	91,6	0,9	6,5	5,4	5,9
5. Great Lakes Countries		**43,3**	**65,6**	**126**			–	–	**146**	**7,8**	–	**–5,7**	**110**	**13,3**	–			
DRC	0,431	35,6	51,5	86	30	59	313	127	110	(5,4)	–1,3	–8,3	(208)	11,2	59,4	142,3	2089	–
Burundi	0,313	5,5	6,8	16	25	46	176	147	140	0,6	2,4	4,2	–1,6	163,3	0,9	3,7	11,8	16,1
Rwanda	0,403	7,2	7,9	24	6	64	321	227	230	1,8	1,6	–3,3	3,1	71,6	1,3	4,0	18,1	16,2
B: **CEFAC** 4+5		**72,7**	**95,0**	**191**			–	–	**280**	**27,0**	–	–	**93**	**35,8**	–			
6. Southern Africa		**94,2**	**105,0**	**221**			–	–	**300**	**42,0**	–	–	**136**	**43**	–			
Angola	0,405	10,0	13,0	27	33	42	698	527	350	8,8	0,6	–6,4	–0,8	213,6	18,7	–	924	708
Botswana	0,572	1,3	1,7	2	49	75	1678	3116	3070	5,2	9,9	1,4	8,5	7,8	0,4	12,0	10,3	10,4
Lesotho	0,535	1,8	2,2	4	26	82	311	486	570	0,9	6,8	0,9	3,5	63,2	0,6	12,8	7,3	9,8
Malawi	0,400	8,8	11,0	24	15	58	169	166	200	1,7	3,2	0,9	–0,4	163,6	2,8	14,6	33,2	33,8
Mozambique	0,322	15,7	20,0	41	38	42	166	–	200	3,7	0,6	3,5	–0,7	198,1	7,4	34,9	41,1	34,9
Tanzania	0,440	27,3	34,0	66	33	73	–	–	210	9,0	0,8	0,4	2,7	82,9	3,1	26,1	24,3	20,9
Zambia	0,433	8,5	9,5	24	40	76	551	388	330	2,9	–1,2	–1,3	1,3	205,3	5,9	38,3	63,5	80,8
Zimbabwe	0,551	9,7	11,7	20	36	87	638	703	690	7,4	1,7	–0,5	–6,7	56	4,1	11,0	21,9	27,0
Namibia	0,610	1,8	1,9	4	31	81	2384	2133	940	3,4	0,6	1,2	1,6	–	–	13,4	10,4	9,9

	HDI value	Population (millions)			Urban population (%)	Adult literacy rate (%)	Real per capita GDP ($)			GDP ($bn)	Annual per capita GNP growth rate (%)			External debt of GNP – $bn (%)		Annual inflation rate (%)		
	2002	1990	2000	2030	2000	1998	1990	1995	1998	2002	1965–1980	1998	2000	2002		1980–1989	1990–1998	2000
7. Indian Ocean		**13,8**	**17,2**	**32**			–	–	**460**	**8,1**	–	–	**97,0**	**7,9**	–	–	–	–
Madagascar	0,469	12,0	15,9	29	30	65	344	238	260	3,8	–0,4	1,5	1,6	123,6	4,6	17,8	22,1	18,7
Mauritius	0,772	1,1	1,3	2	41	84	1802	4034	3740	4,3	3,7	4,0	6,9	54,6	2,4	8,5	6,2	6,9
8. Eastern Africa		**125,1**	**158,4**	**347**			–	–	–	**31,2**	**34.8**	–	–	**97,4**	**33,9**	–	–	–
Kenya	0,513	24,0	30,1	62	34	80	1404	–	350	10,3	3,1	–0,3	–2,6	61,6	6,1	9,0	15,8	15,1
Uganda	0,444	18,8	21,5	51	14	65	–	332	310	6,1	–2,2	3,9	0,8	55,4	3,4	108,1	15,3	10,5
Eritrea	0,421	–	3,8	–	18	52	90	–	175	0,6	–	–	–10,6	44,8	0,3	–	10,1	–
Ethiopia	0,327	49,2	63,0	159	16	36	–	110	100	6,3	0,4	1,0	3,0	86,6	5,5	2,0	8,0	5,3
Somalia	–	7,5	10,0	17	28	24	–	–	–	–	–0,1	–	–	–	–	42,8	–	–
Sudan	0,493	25,2	30,0	57	37	56	229	–	290	11,5	0,8	3,1	6,4	161,4	18,6	–	74,4	81,1
C: **COMESA** 6+7+8		**233,1**	**271,0**	**600**	**22**		–	–	**220**	**84,9**	–	**0,2**	–	**100**	**84,8**			
9. South Africa	**0,695**	**35,3**	**41,0**	**65**	**58**	**85**	**4620**	–	**3310**	**125,9**	**3,2**	**–0,4**	**1,4**	**20,3**	**25,6**	**14,2**	**10,6**	**8,7**
Sub-Saharan Africa	**0,464**	**500**	**645**	**1340**	**45**		**1070**	–	**1520**	**302**	**1,5**	**–0,4**	**1,2**	**82,0**	**247,1**	**21,4**	–	–

Sources: World Bank (2003), UNDP (2000) and African Development Bank (2003) statistics.
Real adjusted GDP is expressed in purchasing power parity and not in official exchange rate terms.
The dollar GDP is obtained by converting national currency GDP to the official exchange rate.
The human development indicator (HDI) (UNDP) is explained on p. 31.

BIBLIOGRAPHY

Adda, J. & Smouts, M-Cl. *La France face au Sud, le mirior brisé*. Karthala, Paris, 1990.

African Development Bank. *African Development Report*. Economica, Paris, 2000.

African Development Bank. *Annual Reports on African Development*. Abidjan.

African Economic Commission (ECA). *Cadre africain de réference pour les programmes d'ajustment structurel en vue du redressement et de la transformation socio-économique*. Addis Ababa, 1989.

Agier, M., Copains, J. & Morice A.(eds.). *Classes ouvrières d'Afrique noire*. Karthala, Paris, 1986.

ALTERSIAL, CERED & ORSTROM. *Nourrir les villes en Afrique subsaharienne*. L'Harmattan, Paris, 1985.

Amin, S. *Impérialisme et sous-développement en Afrique*. Anthropos, Paris, 1976.

Amselle, J-L. & M'Bokolo, E. *Au coeur de l'éthnie. Éthnie, tribalisme et état en Afrique*. La Découverte, Paris, 1986.

Amselle, J-L. *Enchevêtrements*. Paris, 2001.

Annan, K. *The causes of conflicts and the promotion of durable peace and sustainable development in Africa*. Department of the Secretary General of the Security Council, New York, United Nations, 1998.

Arcand, Guillaumont P. & Guillaumont S. "Are policy reforms and growth in Africa sustainable?" *ABCDE Conference Paper*, 2000.

Arts, J.J., Cogneau, D., Herrera, J., De Monchy, G. & Roubaud, F. *L'Économie camarounaise. Un espoir évanoui*. Karthala, Paris.

Assidon, E. *Le commerce captif. Les sociétes commerciales francaises de l'Afrique noire*. L'Harmattan, Paris, 1989.

Assidon, E. & Jaquemot, P. (eds.). *Politique de change et ajustement en Afrique*. Ministry of Co-operation, Paris, 1988.

Azam, J-P. "Marchés parallèles et convertibilité. Analyse théorique avec réference aux économies africaines". *Revue Économique*, No 1, January 1991.

Azam, J-P. "Civil peace and commitment to ethno-regional redistribution in Africa". *ABCDE Conference Paper*, Paris, June 2000.

Babassana, H. *Travail forcé, expropriation et formation du salariat en Afrique noire*. PUG, Grenoble, 1978.

Bach, D. & Kirk-Green, E. (eds.). *États et sociétes en Afrique francophone*. Economica, Paris, 1993.

BAD. *Rapport sur le développement en Afrique*. Economica, Paris, 2003.

Badouin, R. *Systèmes fonciers et développement economique*. Cujas, Paris, 1979.
Balandier, G. *Sociologie actuelle de l'Afrique noire. Dynamique sociale en Afrique centrale*. PUF, Paris, 1971.
Bandt de, J. & Hugon, P. (eds.). *Les Tiers Nations en mal d'industrie*. Economica, Paris, 1988.
Baron, C. *Autonomie, intégration des espaces urbains africains*. Thesis, Bordeaux I, 1994.
Bates, H.B. & Lofchie, M.L. (eds.). *Agricultural development in Africa*. Praeger, New York, 1980.
Bauer, P.T. & Yamey, B.S. *Markets, market control and marketing reform*. Weidenfeld & Nicolson, London, 1969.
Bayart, J-F. *L'État en Afrique. La politique du ventre*. Fayard, Paris, 1989.
Bayart, J-F. Hibou, B. & Ellis, C. *La criminalisation des états en Afrique*. Paris, Complexe, 1997.
Becker, C. & Morrisson, A. *Beyond urban bias: African cities in an era of structural adjustment*. University of Colorado, Boulder, mimeo, 1990.
Bekolo-Ebe, Touna-Mama & Owoudi, F. *Les économies africaines face à l'Europe de 1993*. Yaoundé, Presses Universitaires du Cameroun, 1993.
Berg, E. (ed.). *Accelerated development in sub-Saharan Africa*. World Bank, Washington, 1981.
Berg, R.J. & Whitaker, J.S. *Stratégies pour le développement africain*. Economica, Paris, 1989.
Bernstein, H. & Campbell B.K. (eds.). *Contradictions of accumulation in Africa. Studies in economy and state*. Sage, Beverly Hills, 1985.
Berry, S. *Fathers work for their sons, accumulation, mobility and class formation in an extended Yoruba community*. California University Press, Los Angeles, 1985.
Berthelemy, J-C. & Söderling, M. *L'Afrique émergente*. OCDE Development Assistance Centre, Paris, 2001.
Berthelemy, J-C. (ed.). *Quel avenir pour l'économie africaine?* OCDE, Paris, 1995.
Berthelemy, J-C. & Morrisson, C. "Pénurie de devises et crise de l'agriculture commerciale en Afrique subsaharienne". *Économie et prévision*, No 97, 1991.
Berthelemy, J-C. & Söderling, L. *The role of capital accumulation. Adjustment and structural change for economic take-off: empirical evidence from Africa growth episodes*. mimeo, OCDE Development Assistance Centre, Paris, 1999.
Bertrand, H. *Le Congo, formation sociale et mode de développement économique*. Maspero, Paris, 1975.
Bevan, L., Bigsten, A., Collier, P. & Gunning, J.W. "Peasant supply response in rationed economies". *World Development*, Volume 15, No 4, 1987.
Bloom, D. & Sachs, J. "Geography, demography and economic growth in Africa". *Brookings Paper in Economic Activity*, September 1998.
Bohannan, P. & Dalton, G. (eds.). *Markets in Africa*. North Western University Press, [S.L.], 1962.
Bomsel, O. *Dynamiques économiques des pays miniers et instabilités des matières premières minérales*. CERNA, Paris, 1985.
Bourguignon, F. & Morrisson, C. *Ajustement et équité dans les pays en développement. Une approche nouvelle*. OCDE, Paris, 1992.
Bugnicourt, J. *Disparités régionales et aménagement du territoire en Afrique*. A. Collin, Paris, 1971.
Capet, M. *Traite d'économie tropicale: les économies d'AOF*. R. Pichon and Durand-Aujas, Paris, 1958.
CEPII. *Économie mondiale 1990–2000: l'impératif de la croissance*. Economica, Paris, 1992.
CEA. *Economic Report on Africa*. Addis Ababa, 1999.

Cerruti, P., Hugon, P. & Collignon, S. *La coopération monétaire en Afrique subsaharienne: le rôle des arrangements régionaux de paiements.* CEE, December 1992.

Chalmin, P. "L'Afrique dans le jeu alimentaire mondial". *Politique Africaine,* No 37, October 1990.

Charmes, J. "Une revue critique des concepts, définition et recherces sur le secteur informel". In Turnham et al. *Nouvelles approches du secteur informel.* OCDE, Paris, 1990.

Chavagneux, T. & Ghana, C. *Une révolution de bon sens. Économie politique de l'ajustement.* Karthala, Paris, 1997.

Cling, J.P. *L'Économie sud-africaine au sortir de l'apartheid.* Karthala, Paris, 2000.

CNUCED. *Capital Flows and Growth in Africa.* New York and Genève, 2000.

CNUCED. *Les Pays les moins avancés.* Report 2000, United Nations, New York, 2000.

Collier, P. & Gunning, J.W. "Explaining African economic performance". *Journal of Economic Literature,* Volume 37, pp. 64–111, 1999.

Collier, P. & Hoeffler, A. "On the economic causes of civil wars". *Oxford Economic Papers,* Volume 50, pp. 563–73, 2000.

Commission Économique pour L'Afrique (CEA). *Cadre africain de référence pour les programmes d'ajustement structurel en vue du redressement el de la transformation socio-économique.* Addis Ababa, 1989.

Coquery-Vidrovitch, C. *Afrique noire. Permanences et ruptures.* Payot, Paris, 1989.

Cornia, G.A., Jolly, R. & Stewart, F. *Structural adjustment with a human face: protecting vulnerable groups.* UNICEF, Economica, Paris, 1987.

Cornia, G.A. & Helleiner, G.K. (eds.). *From Adjustment to Development in Africa.* MacMillan Press, London, 1996.

Cour, J-M. *et al. Études des perspectives à long terme de l'Afrique de l'Ouest. Pour penser l'avenir de l'Afrique de l'Ouest. Une vision à long terme.* OCDE, Sahel Club, Paris, 1992.

Coussy, J. "Economique et politiques de développement". In Coulon, C. & Martin, D. (eds.). *Les Afriques politiques.* La Découverte, Paris, 1991.

Coussy, J. & Hugon, P. (eds.). *Intégration régionale et ajustement structurel en Afrique subsaharienne.* Ministry of Development and Co-operation, Paris, 1991.

Coussy, J. & Vallin, J. (eds.). *Crise et population en Afrique.* CEPED, Paris, 1996.

Couty, P., Pontie, P. & Robineau, B. *Le développement: idéologie et pratique.* ORSTOM, Paris, 1983.

Deblé, I. & Hugon, P. (eds.). *Vivre et survivre dans les villes africaines.* PUF, Paris, 1981.

De Bandt, J. & Hugon, P. (eds.). *Les tiers nations et mal d'industrie.* Economica, Paris, 1988.

Devarajan, S. & De Melo, J. "Evaluating participation in the African Monetary Union. A statistical analysis of the CFA zone". *World Bank Development,* Vol 1, No 15 (4), 1986.

Devarajan, S., Easterly, W.R. & Pack, H. "Is investment in Africa too low or too high? Macro and micro evidence". *Journal of African Economics,* 2001.

Diouf, M. *L'Intégration économique en Afrique de l'Ouest,* Publisud, Paris, 1986.

Dubresson, A. & Raison, J-P. *L'Afrique subsaharienne, une géographie du changement.* Paris, A. Colin, 1998.

Dumont, R. *L'Afrique noire est mal partie.* Le Seuil, Paris, 1962.

Dupriez, G. *La Formation des salaries en Afrique.* Drukkerij Frankie, Louvain, 1973.

Dupuy, C.I. & Servet, J.M. "Pratiques informelles d'épargne et de pret. L'exemple sénégalais". *Économie et humanisme,* No 294, March/April, 1987.

Durufle, G. *L'Ajustement structurel en Afrique (Sénégal, Côte-d'Ivoire, Madagascar)*. Karthala, Paris, 1988.
Easterly, W. & Levine, R. *Africa's growth tragedy*. World Bank, Washington, 1995.
Ellis, S. & Fauré, Y-A. *Entreprises et entrepreneurs africains*. Karthala, Paris, 1995.
Elunga. *L'Afrique a-t-elle besoin d'un ajustement culturel?* Karthala, Paris, 1990.
Engelhardt, P. *L'Afrique miroir du monde?* Paris, Arléa, 1998.
Esseks, J. (ed.). *L'Afrique de l'indépendance politique à l'indépendance économique*. Maspero, Paris, 1975.
Fauré, Y-A. & Médard, J-F. (eds.). *État et bourgeoisie en Côte-d'Ivoire*. Karthala, Paris, 1982.
Faure, Y-A. & Labazée, P. *Dispositif d'appui au secteur privé en Côte-d'Ivoire et au Burkina Faso*. IRD/Karthala, Paris, 2000.
Faveraeau, O. "La question du développement et l'économie des conventions". In Hugon *et al.*, 1994.
Ferguson, J.N. *The Anti Politics Machine, Development Depolitization and Bureaucraty in Lesotho*. University of Minesota Press, Minesota, 1990.
Fontaine, J-M. (ed.) *Réformes du commerce extérieur et politique de développement*. PUF, in collaboration with *Tiers Monde*, Paris, 1991.
Fortes, M. & Evans Pritchard, E.E. *Systèmes politiques africains*. PUF, Paris, 1964.
Fotorino, E., Guillemin, C. & Orsenna, E. *Besoins d'Afrique*. Fayard, Paris, 1992.
Gabas, J-J. *De l'aide à l'investissement au soutien financier*. Club du Sahel/OCDE, Paris, 1990.
Gagey, F. *Comprendre l'économie africaine (textes choisis)*. L'Harmattan, Paris, 1985.
Gastellu, J-M. *Mais où sont ces unités économiques que nos amis recherchent tant en Afrique?* Stateco, Paris, 1979.
Gemdev. *La Convention de Lomé en question*. Karthala, Paris, 1998.
Gentil, D. & Hugon, P. (eds.). Le financement décentralisé. Special Edition of *Tiers Monde*, Development Assistance Centre Vol 37, No 145, January–March, 1996.
Gérardin, H. *La zone franc*. L'Harmattan, Paris, 1989.
Géronimi, V. *Le "Syndrome hollandais" dans les économies du golfe de Guinée*. Thesis, Paris-X-Nanterre, 1992.
Giri, J. *L'Afrique en panne. Vingt-cinq ans de développement*. Karthala, Paris, 1986.
Giri, J. *Le Sahel au XXIe siècle. Un essai de réflexion prospective en sociétés sahéliennes*. Paris, Karthala, 1989.
Goreux, L-M. *La Dévaluation du FCFA. Un premier bilan*. World Bank, 1995.
Grégoire, L-J. *Le Zimbabwe. Évolution économique et perspectives*. L'Harmattan, Paris, 1989.
Grellet, G. *Les structures économiques de l'Afrique noire*. PUF, Paris, 1982.
Griffon, M. *Prospectives agricoles africaines*. CIRAD, Ron, 2001.
Guillaumont, P. (ed.). *Croissance et ajustement. Les problèmes de l'Afrique de l'Ouest*. Economica, Paris, 1985.
Guillaumont, P. & Guillaumont, S. (eds.). *Stratégies de développement comparées: zone franc et hors zone franc*. Economica, Paris, 1988.
Guillaumont, P., Guillaumont, S. & Plane, P. *Comparaison de l'efficacité des politiques d'ajustment en Afrique: zone franc et hors zone franc*. CCCE, roneo, Paris, 1991.
Guillaumont, P. & Guillaumont, S. (eds.). *Ajustement et développement dans les pays ACP*. Economica, Paris, 1994.
Guillaumont, P. & Combe, P. "Instabilités et performances des économies africaines". *ABCDE Conference Paper*, 2000.
Harris, J. & Todaro, M. "Migration, unemployment and development: a two sector analysis". *American Economic Review*, March 1970.
Hayek, F. *Droit, législation, liberté*. Le Seuil, Paris, 1980.

Helleiner, G. *Capital account regime and the developing countries*. MacMillan Press, Basingstoke, 1999.
Henry, A. et al. *La Société des amis*. CCCE, roneo, Paris, 1990.
Herskovits, M.J. & Horowitz (eds.). *Economic transition in Africa*. London, 1964.
Hibou, B. *L'Afrique est-elle protectionniste?* Karthala, Paris, 1997.
Hirschman, A.O. *Exit, Voice and Loyalty: response to Decline in Firms, Organizations and States*, Cambridge, Harvard University Press 1970; translation, *Face au déclin des entreprises et des institutions*, Ed. Ouvrières, Paris, 1982.
Hugon, P. *Analyse du sous-développement en Afrique noire*. PUF, Paris, 1968.
Hugon, P. et al. *La petite producteur marchande et l'emploi dans le secteur informel africain*. IEDES, Paris, 1977.
Hugon, P. (ed.). "Les Africains de l'an 2000". *Afrique Contemporaine*, No 146, second trimester, 1988.
Hugon, P., Coussy, J. & Sudrie, O. *Urbanisation et dépendance alimentaire en Afrique subsaharienne*. SEDES, Paris, 1989.
Hugon, P. "Les politiques d'ajustement structurel". In *Encyclopédie économique*, Economica, Paris, 1990.
Hugon, P. & Sudrie, O. *L'Ajustement dans les ACP*. European Parliament Study, 1992.
Hugon, P., Pourcet, G. & Quiers-Valette, S. (eds.). *L'Afrique des incertitudes*. Paris, PUF, 1994.
Hugon, P. & Sudrie, O. (eds.). *La prospective africaine*. MAE/CERED Report, Paris, roneo, three volumes, 2000.
Hugon, P. *La zone franc a l'heure de l'euro*. Karthala, Paris, 1999.
Hugon, P. (ed.). *Analyse comparée de l'intégration régionale*. Paris, MAE, 2001.
Hugon, P. (ed.). *Les Économies en développement à l'heure de la régionalisation*. Karthala, Paris, 2003.
Hussain, H. *Exorcism of the Ghost: An alternative growth model for measuring the financing gap*. BAD, Abidjan, 2000.
Hyden, G. *Beyond ujamaa in Tanzania: underdevelopment and the uncaptured peasantry*. University of California Press, Berkeley, 1980.
Igue, J. *Le Territoire et l'État. Les dimensions spatiales du développement*. Karthala, Paris,1994.
Iliffe, J. *Les Africains. Histoire d'un continent*. Aubier-Flammarion, Paris, 1997.
ISTED. *Dynamique de l'urbanisation de l'Afrique au sud du Sahara*. Ministry of Cooperation, Paris, 1996.
Jaquemot, P. & Raffinot, M. *Accumulation et développement. Dix études sur les économies du tiers monde*. L'Harmattan, Paris, 1986.
Ki Zerbo. *Histoire de l'Afrique noire d'hier à demain*. Hatier, Paris, 1980.
Kodjo, E. *Et demain l'Afrique*. Stock, Paris, 1985.
Koulibaly, M. *Le Libéralisme, chance pour l'Afrique*. L'Harmattan, Paris, 1992.
Lachaud, J-P. & Penouil, M. *Le Développement spontané*. Pendone, Paris, 1986.
Lachaud, J-P. *Pauvreté et inégalités, contribution à l'analyse spatiale*. CED, Bordeaux IV, Series Number 4, 2000.
Laporte, B. *Intégration économique régionale et échanges commerciaux en Afrique de l'Ouest*. Thesis, CERDI, Clermont-Ferrand, 1996.
Latouche, S. *L'Autre Afrique. Entre don et marché*. Albin Michel, Paris, 1998.
Lebris, E., Leindorfer, E. & Leroy, E. *Enjeux, fonciers en Afrique noire*. Karthala, Paris, 1982.
Lelart, M. (ed.). *La Tontine, pratique informelle d'épargne et de crédit dans des pays en développement*. John Libbey, Paris, 1990.
Lele, U. *Agricultural growth domestic policies. The external environment and assistance to Africa*. World Bank, Washington DC, 1989.
Leroy, E., Karsenty, A. & Bertrand, A. *La Sécurisation en Afrique. Pour une gestion des ressources renouvelables*. Karthala, Paris, 1996.

Leys, C. *Underdevelopment in Kenya: The political economy of Neo-Colonialism.* Heinemann, London, 1975.

L'Hériteau, M.F. & Chavagneux C. *Le Fonds monétaire international et le tiers monde.* PUF, Paris, second edition, 1995.

Lipton, M. *Why the poor stay poor: A study of urban bias in world development.* Temple Smith, London, 1977.

Magnard, F. & Tenzer, N. *La Crise africaine: quelle politique de coopération pour la France?* PUF, Paris, 1988.

Mahieu, R. *Les Fondements de la crise économique en Afrique.* L'Harmattan, Paris, 1990.

Mainguy, C. *La Compétitivité extérieure de l'Afrique subsaharienne: le rôle des politiques économiques.* Karthala, Paris, 1988.

Maldant, B., Haubert, M. & Breton, Y. *Croissance et conjoncture dans l'Ouest africain.* PUF, Paris, 1973.

Marie, A. (ed.). *L'Afrique des individus.* Karthala, Paris, 1999.

Marseille, J. *Empire colonial et capitalisme français. Histoire d'un divorce.* Albin Michel, Paris, 1984.

Mbembé, A. *De la post-colonie.* Karthala, Paris, 2000.

Médard, J-F. (ed.). *États d'Afrique noire. Formations, mécanismes et crise.* Karthala, Paris, 1991.

Meier, G.M. & Steel, W. (eds.). *Industrial djustment in sub-Saharan Africa.* Oxford University Press, Oxford, 1989.

Meillassoux, C. *Femmes, greniers, capitaux.* Maspero, Paris, 1975.

Michailof, S. (ed.). *La France et l'Afrique. Vade-mecum pour un nouveau voyage.* Karthala, Paris, 1993.

Michaelet, C-A. (ed.). *Le Défi du développement indépendant.* Rochevignes, Paris, 1983.

Mkandawire, T. & Saluda, C. *Our continent, our future; African perspectives on structural adjustment.* Trenton, New Jersey, Asnara, Africa World Press, 1999.

Monga, C. & Tchatchouang, J-C. *Sortir du piège monétaire.* Economica, Paris, 1996.

Naudet, M. *Une analyse du degré d'ouverture internationale.* OCDE, Sahel Club, Paris, 1994.

Nuadet, J.D. *Trouver les problèmes aux solutions.* OCDE, Paris, 1999.

Ntamatungiro. *Stabilisation des recettes d'exportation. Stock régulateur, contrat à terme, options.* Economica, Paris, 1988.

O'Connell, S.A. & Ndulu, B.J. Africa's growth experience: a focus on sources of growth. *Working Paper,* 2000.

Olivier de Sardan, J-P. *Anthropologie et développement.* Karthala, Paris, 1995.

ONUDI. Industrial development report. Vienna, 2002–2003.

Ouali, K.S. *Intégration et développement.* Economica, Paris, 1990.

Pélissier, P. *Les Paysans du Sénégal.* Fabrèque, Saint-Yriex, 1967.

PNUD. Report on human development. New York, 1997 and 2000.

Pourcet, B. *La Dynamique du sous-développement à Madagascar.* Thesis, Paris-Nanterre, 1979.

Quiers-Valette, S. "Les investissements directs étrangers: du risque à la 'certitude negative'". In Hugon, Pourcet & Quiers-Valette, 1994.

Raffinot, M. *Ajustement et endettement dans les pays en développement.* AUPELF, UREF, Paris, 1992.

Raffinot, M. & Moisseron, D. *Dette et pauvreté.* Economica, Paris, 2000.

Raison, J-P. *Les hautes terres de Madagascar.* ORSTOM, Karthala, Paris, 1984.

Ravenhill, J. (ed.). *Africa in economic crisis.* Columbia University Press, New York, 1988.

Requier-Desjardins, D. *L'alimentation en Afrique: manger ce qu'on peut produire*. Karthala, Paris, 1989.

Rey, P-H. *Colonialisme, néo-colonialisme et transition au capitalisme, exemple de la "Camilog" au Congo, Brazzaville*. Maspero, Paris, 1971.

Robson, P. *Intégration, développement et équité en Afrique de l'Ouest*. Economica, Paris, 1987.

Rose, T. (ed.). *Afrique subsaharienne: de la crise au redressement*. OCDE, Paris, 1985.

Sachs, J. & Wagner, A.M. "Sources of African economic growth". *Journal of African Economics*, Volume 6 (3), 1997.

Sall, A. (ed.). *La Compétitivité future des économies africaines*. Futures Africains, Karthala, Paris, 2000.

Sautter, G. *De l'Atlantique au fleuve Congo: une géographie du sous-peuplement*. Mouton, Volume 2, Paris, 1966.

Schulders, G. *S'unir: L'intégration en Afrique centrale*. L'Harmattan, Paris, 1990.

Sen, A.K. *Poverty and famines: an essay on entitlements and deprivation*. Clarendon Press, Oxford, 1981.

Severino, J.M. & Servant, P. *Conjoncture des États d'Afrique et de l'océan Indien*. Ministry of Co-operation, Paris, 1992.

Sindzingre, A. "Crédibilité des États et économie politique des réformes en Afrique". *Economie et sociétés*, Series P98.

Stiglitz. *La grande désillusion*. Fayard, Paris, 2002.

Stewart, F., Lall, S. & Wangwe, S. (eds.). *Alternative development strategies in sub-Saharan Africa*. MacMillan, London, 1992.

Suret-Canale, J. *Afrique noire occidentale et centrale*. Éditions Sociales, three volumes, Paris, 1977.

Tapinos, G., Hugon, P. & Vimard, P. (eds.). *La Côte-d'Ivoire à l'aube du XXIe siècle*. Karthala, Paris, 2001.

Terray, E. (ed.). *L'État contemporain en Afrique*. L'Harmattan, Paris, 1987.

Thomas, L.V. *Le Socialisme et l'Afrique*. Le Livre Africain, Paris, 1966.

UNESCO. *General History of Africa*, UNESCO/NEA, Volume 8, Paris, 1980–1990.

Valleé, O. *Le prix de l'argent CFA. Heurs et malheurs de la zone franc*. Karthala, Paris, 1989.

Vallée, O. & Missen, F. *Gemnocratie, l'économie politique du diamant en Afrique*. Desclée de Brouwer, Bruxelles, 1999.

Van der Hooven, R. & Van der Kraai, J. *L'Ajustement structurel et au-delà en Afrique subsaharienne*. Karthala, Paris, 1994.

Vinokur, A. "Les systèmes éducatifs et leur régulation". *Afrique contemporaine*, No 172, 1994.

Von Braun, Teklu, J., Chavagneux, T. & Ghana, C. *Une revolution de bon sens. Economie politique de l'ajustement*. Karthala, Paris, 1997.

Winter, G. (ed.). *Inégalités et politiques publiques en Afrique*. Karthala, Paris, 2001.

World Bank. *From crisis to sustainable development, from crisis to sustainable growth* (Lendell Mills, P., Agarwala, R. & Please, S.), Washington DC, 1989.

World Bank. *World Development Report*. Washington, 1991a.

World Bank. *Adjustment lending revisited, policies to restore growth*. Washington, 1991b.

World Bank. *Can Africa claim the 21st century*. Washington DC, 2000.

World Bank. *Attacking Poverty*. Washington DC, 2000.

World Bank. *A continent in transition: sub-Saharan Africa in the mid-1990s*. Africa region, Washington DC, 1995.

Young, C. *The African colonial state in comparative perspective*. Yale University Press, New Haven, 1994.

INDEX